"Authentic. Informative. God-honoring. Flake's *Tears to Joy* is an amazing resource for those seeking relief from the suffering and heartache that often accompany mental illness. I certainly plan to recommend it to my patients and their family members."

—Branko Radulovacki, MD, Psychiatrist in private practice, Founder of FaithWorks, NAMI (National Alliance on Mental Illness) Exemplary Psychiatrist Award 2010, 2009, MHA (Mental Health America) Heroes in the Fight Award 2009, Atlanta Magazine Top Doctor 2011, 2010, 2009, 2007

"Natalie Flake has written a passionate text that will serve to both educate and inspire all who read it. In an authentic voice, she demonstrates the vulnerabilities of those who are companions, spouses, and caregivers of those with serious mental illness. Yet, while she illuminates the pain of mental illness, she also uplifts her readers by providing them sources of hope and healing."

—Holly A. Haynes, (EdD, Harvard University in Human Development & Psychology), Associate Professor, Behavioral Sciences, Truett-McConnell College

Tears TO JOY

Tears to JOY

Finding Hope in the Presence
of Bipolar Disorder and Suicide

NATALIE FLAKE

TATE PUBLISHING
AND ENTERPRISES, LLC

Published by Tate Publishing & Enterprises, LLC
127 E. Trade Center Terrace | Mustang, Oklahoma 73064 USA
1.888.361.9473 | www.tatepublishing.com

Tate Publishing is committed to excellence in the publishing industry. The company reflects the philosophy established by the founders, based on Psalm 68:11,
"The Lord gave the word and great was the company of those who published it."

Published in the United States of America

ISBN: 978-1-62147-389-3
1. Psychology / Psychopathology / Bipolar Disorder
2. Biography & Autobiography / Personal Memoirs
12.08.27

DEDICATION

This book is dedicated to Michael Flake, for the glory of God and the inspiration of others.

ACKNOWLEDGEMENTS

Special thanks to:

Helen First Baptist Church, for being the hands and feet of Jesus in my life.

Deirdre, Leah, Matt, Pastor Jim, and Selena, for sharing your hearts through letters.

Cheryl Lewis, for helping me to turn this dream into a reality. I thank God for you, dear sister!

Jane Flake, for the gift of your son. He truly was a treasure!

Brooney (Doug Pope), for standing by me during the good times and the bad.

My daddy, Randy Pope, for feeding my passion to write since I was a child.

My mom and stepdad, Hershell and Kaye Guthrie, for always believing in me.

Jorjanne Flake, for being my greatest cheerleader and an incredible blessing!

TABLE OF CONTENTS

INTRODUCTION

There are stretches in life when you feel as though all of your dreams have come true. You are surrounded by people you love. You have a great job. You adore your spouse. In short, things just couldn't get much better. Then there are times when life throws you a vicious curve ball. Nothing makes sense. Everything that once was vibrant and alive becomes desperate and hollow.

In my mid-twenties, I was living the American dream. All of life's best seemed to be coming my way. My husband, Michael, and I were looking forward to growing a family and serving the Lord overseas. I couldn't have asked for more, but I had no idea how far we were about to plunge.

Overnight, it seemed, my husband began to experience severe mood swings. He was eventually diagnosed with bipolar disorder. Our lives became a constant roller coaster of highs and lows. Michael descended into severe depression and saw no hope for relief. His agony led him to attempt suicide. Tragically, he eventually succeeded. My heart was utterly broken, and I didn't know where to turn. It felt as though God had surely abandoned me; he seemed to answer my cries with silence. My family and friends wanted to help but didn't know how. In short, my fairytale had become a nightmare from which I couldn't wake up.

This book is for those who are hurting and feel alone and hopeless. It is also for those who want to help. Through our struggles with Michael's mental illness and his eventual suicide, I learned that only one thing is certain in life: God is who he says he is. I've realized that God is a good God, that he is sovereign, and that he loves us. This may sound contradictory, but it was this truth that gave me courage to continue when I wondered if I could go on. There were times when I screamed at the Lord in anger and asked, "Why, Lord? Why me?" While I never received a direct answer to my questions, he gave me a far greater gift—*his presence.*

If you or someone you know is hurting, I pray that you, too, will find the hope and peace that only comes from Christ. I want to believe that my experience (which is ultimately more about God than about me) will inspire you to cling to the promises of his Word. When you don't understand, seek the face of God. He will give you the strength to weather your own trials with courage and hope.

Exposing my personal loss is painful, but by sharing what happened, I want to undermine the stigma associated with mental illness. Fear of rejection prevents millions from getting the help they need to recover. Research suggests that one in four adults suffers from a mental disorder.[1] Truly, mental illness is a disease that affects people from every walk of life. Many of you know someone with a psychological disorder. You may be like those of my friends who longed to help, but didn't know how. This book will suggest some practical ways that you can support your loved one.

Finally, if you understand intimately what I am describing because you are navigating your way toward recovery, take heart. No matter how bleak you may feel, your disorder does not define who you are. God has a perfect plan for your life.

> "For I know the plans I have for you," declares the Lord, "Plans to prosper you and not to harm you, plans to give you hope and a future. Then you will call on me and come and pray to me, and I will listen to you. You will seek me and find me when you seek me with all your heart. I will be found by you," declares the Lord, "And will bring you back from captivity."[2]

CHAPTER 1

When I arrived home that day, I saw the red light blinking on the answering machine. I pushed play and listened as my husband's voice entered the room.

"Natalie, I just wanted to tell you how much I love you," said Michael. "No matter what happens, I love you. You mean so much to me, and I wish I could be a better husband to you. Tell Jorjanne that her daddy loves her and always will. I love you. Bye."

I stood there, shuddering, with clouds of confusion cluttering my mind. I replayed the message and tears filled my eyes. Was my husband trying to communicate something deeper?

Was he trying to tell me good-bye?

His depression had been more severe lately, but I had noticed no signs that he might become suicidal again.

I grabbed the phone and punched in his number, anxiously waiting as it continued to ring. I shifted my weight and cried out to God, "Lord, please let him answer!"

At last, I heard a mumbled, "Hello."

Yes! He answered! I rejoiced inwardly.

"Michael, where are you?" I asked, trying to keep my voice calm.

"I'm in Blairsville. I just left one of the churches here," Michael mumbled. A million questions raced through my mind, but the only ones I could formulate were "Which church? Why are you there?"

"I came to pray. It's one of the churches I've spoken at before. I can't remember the name of it," Michael said.

"Where are you now?"

"Driving. I'm going into the woods. What did the doctor say about Jorjanne?" He asked, trying to change the subject.

Seemed like every time one of us went to the doctor, it was always the same. "Sinus infection."

"Let me talk to her," he blurted out with a sigh.

"But I need to talk to you. I have something to ask you." I couldn't imagine why he wanted to talk with Jorjanne.

"No. I need to talk to her. I need to tell her that I love her," Michael replied.

"She knows that. First, let's talk." I thought if I could just get him to open up and tell me what he was feeling, I could make it all better. Michael's frustrations were growing as he huffed, "Please put Jorjanne on the phone."

"Okay, I'll put her on the phone, but I want to talk with you when you finish talking to her."

Timidly, Jorjanne answered the phone.

"Hello."

"Jorjanne, this is Daddy. I just want you to know that I love you. You know that, right? Daddy loves you and will always love you. You are so special to me, and I am very proud of you. Be a good girl and remember that I love you." Michael's words were so rushed, as if his very life depended on Jorjanne knowing how much he cared.

"Okay, Daddy. I love you, too. Here's Mommy."

Snatching the phone from Jorjanne I cried into the phone, "Michael?"

"Yeah?" he answered.

"I don't know how to ask you this, and I really don't want to ask it, but I have to. Are you about to do something stupid?" There. I'd finally done it. I asked him the one question that had been chiming in my mind ever since I'd heard the message on the answering machine. Shifting my weight, and gritting my teeth, I waited for his answer.

"Natalie, I can't take it anymore. I'm so tired of living like this," Michael uttered with a long sigh. "The mood swings are killing me, and I can't be the husband you need. You need more than me. You can do better. I know you'll be okay."

What was he trying to tell me? Life had surely been tough, but we'd survived in the past, and we could do it again. Confident that I could convince him to come home, I said, "Michael, what I need is you. Please, promise me you won't do anything stupid. Just tell me where you are, and I'll come to you. We can face this together." Unfortunately, he needed time.

"I just need to get away and think. I won't do anything stupid. I just need to hear from God. I don't understand why I can't get over this. I feel so bad."

Pleading with him, I begged him to reconsider.

"Please come home. I love you, Michael. I need you. Jorjanne needs you."

Michael needed time alone, time to think.

"I love you both. I need to go. I'll call you later."

And with that, he hung up. I collapsed on the floor in tears.

"Oh, God! What is happening? Protect my baby! Don't let anything happen to him. Give me wisdom! Tell me what to do."

It was not the first time I had prayed this prayer. In fact, during the past five years of our nine-year marriage, I had gotten used to my husband's extreme mood swings—if such a thing is possible. He had been diagnosed with bipolar disorder a year after his normally effervescent personality had become erratic and unstable. We had weathered many, many ups and downs, and over time, his highs and lows had grown more intense.

It was not the first time I feared he would take his own life. Indeed, just months before, he had been hospitalized after what seemed to be an intentional overdose of prescription medication.

But he had survived.

We had survived.

As far as I was concerned, we would again.

How could our life together that began as such a fairy tale have gotten tangled into such a nightmare?

CHAPTER 2

My wedding day had been the best of my life. All the emotions that every young girl feels when she is about to face the man of her dreams at the altar swirled through me. I clearly remember feeling anxious as I stood outside the doors to the church. I was a bit overwhelmed by the huge step I was about to take. My mom, with tears streaming down her cheeks, whispered into my ear, "I love you." As the doors swept open, I saw my beloved at the front of the church.

My two dads (my daddy and my stepdad) escorted me down the aisle. I felt as if I was dreaming. I glanced around me and was amazed by the love in the room. My heart smiled as I saw all my friends and family who had come to share this special day with me.

It seemed surreal that, in moments, I would become Michael's wife. I was only twenty-one and never dreamed that I'd walk this path so early in life. I had always thought I would be much older, with multiple degrees on the wall, before I took this step.

God had other plans, it seemed, and I was giddy. After this day, my life would be forever changed. God, in His sovereignty, had brought Michael and me together. This was truly one of the happiest days of my life. As the music continued to play, I held my head high and glided to the front of the church to my groom.

It seemed like only yesterday that our paths had first crossed. Yes, I had long known who he was—everybody knew Michael. We both attended Mercer University in Macon, Georgia. He was Mr. BSU (Baptist Student Union) and I was an RUF (Reformed University Fellowship) girl. I'd always thought he was a cool guy, but we had never really talked until one fateful day in the cafeteria. We had both walked through the entrance at the same time, and he looked at me, then asked, "Where are you sitting?"

My answer was swift and surprised even me. "Wherever you are," I said, matter-of-factly.

Whoa, Natalie. Slow down, I said to myself. What was I thinking? Being forward was utterly unlike me, but I felt filled with courage when he smiled into my eyes.

We sat our books on a table and were walking toward the buffet line when Michael smiled at me and asked, "What are you doing this weekend?" My hopes surged. Yet, his question could not have been timed worse since, at that very instant, my friend Daryl walked up.

Overhearing the question, Daryl leaned over and said, "She's going to formal with me."

Oh, no! I was mortified. Michael would surely get the wrong impression, though Daryl and I were only friends. Sure enough, Michael looked at me with those great, big eyes, and said, "It's ok. You can sit with Daryl if you'd like. I understand." I assured him I wanted to sit with him, saying, "Oh no. We're just friends. I'd like to sit with you." I couldn't believe I'd just been so bold!

Over lunch, we learned a lot about each other and discovered things in common. We both wanted to go to seminary. In fact, I had just come back from visiting Covenant Seminary in St. Louis, and he was going to visit Southeastern Baptist Theological Seminary that weekend.

He expressed, "There is another school that I'd really like to go and visit, but it is a long drive. I really don't want to drive that far by myself." Curious, I asked, "Where?"

"Southwestern Seminary in Texas," he proclaimed. I was shocked to learn that he wanted to visit the same school I did. When I shared with him about my desire to visit there he asserted, "Well then, we should go together!" I quickly agreed, although I never expected it to actually happen.

In just a few short days, Michael began calling the school, arranging for our visit. I couldn't believe we were really going to do this. I knew who Michael was, but I did not "*know* him, know him." Then came the hard part: telling my parents that I wanted to drive cross country with a guy they had never met. They decided to come and visit, so they could meet this man who wanted to drive to Texas with me, and we all went to lunch. They got along great and, with my parents' blessings, we continued to prepare for our trip. In just a few weeks, we began the incredibly long journey from Georgia to Texas.

I had no idea this would be a life-changing adventure! Michael later told me that he knew he would come back from this trip either really liking me or really hating me. Spending so much time together in a car would be a great litmus test! It didn't take long for us to realize that our commonalities ran deep, and so did our budding affection for each other.

Time flew by as we trekked across the country. As we crossed the mighty Mississippi, Michael became very animated!

"I have the perfect song for this part of our trip!" Michael proudly announced. He even pulled the car over and dug through his cassettes in order to find the "perfect" song. He exclaimed, "Now, just listen. I am so excited! This song is just for our trip."

Nodding expectantly, I replied, "Ok, let's hear it!" Music filled my car, along with these lyrics:

> She's got one big breast in the middle of her chest and eyes in the middle of her nose.
>
> So says I, if you look her in the eye, you'll end up looking up her nose.

"What are you trying to say, Michael Flake?" I asked.

Hysterically laughing, he apologized profusely. "I am so sorry. That's the wrong song!"

We laughed until our sides hurt. From the soundtrack of *Big River*, he had mistakenly cued the tape for "The Royal Nonesuch" instead of "Arkansas." He never lived that down.

Our visit to the seminary passed swiftly, and on the drive back to Georgia, we began to share our hopes and dreams with each other. That time together launched a season of growing closer and closer, until we began seeing each other exclusively. He embodied many of the qualities I found endearing and crucial to a serious relationship.

Not only was Michael romantic, but he was also a man of God. One of the things that impressed me most about him was his knowledge of the Scriptures and his intimate relationship with the Father. We spent many nights talking about the Lord, praying together, and reading the Word together. One of my fondest memories was an evening when Michael opened the Scriptures in my Mercer apartment and began to share with me about the sacrificial system in the Old Testament. He made Scripture come alive and left me longing for more. This was a "Wow!" moment, since it was likely this characteristic more than any other that attracted me to Michael Flake.

As graduation day approached, I found myself on an emotional seesaw. How would I ever live without Michael? We had shared some great times at Mercer, and that chapter of my life was quickly coming to a close. I didn't want it to end. A long-distance relationship would never last. We would never make it. We would both make promises to each other that we couldn't keep. We'd do our best to make it work, but it wouldn't. It couldn't. I found myself both pulling away and drawing closer to Michael at the same time.

Had I known what Michael wrote in his journal this same week, I would have been giddy!

May 29, 1996

I'm in love! But cannot tell her! I love her more than I can describe. With everything in me, I love her. I wrote her a note telling her this.

He waited an entire month before sharing the note with me.

Again, time was the enemy. I found myself with a kaleidoscope of emotions on the day of graduation. I was thrilled to think of what the future might hold, and yet I was also terrified. My feelings for Michael were even more troubling. Why was I so upset about leaving him? By leaving Mercer, I was leaving Michael. Why did that bother me so much? Did I love him? Dare I even go there? I'd been ever so careful to guard my heart. Why did it ache so much at thoughts of us parting company?

After graduation, Daddy and my brother agreed to follow me home with a load of my stuff. I went to a graduation party with Michael and then stopped by to tell Daddy I'd be ready soon. I sat in the car with Michael and experienced the greatest heartache I'd ever had in my life.

Finally, I told Michael that I would see him later and then I cried the entire two and a half hour trip home, bemoaning the fact that I would *not* see him later. His journal mirrored my feelings.

June 10, 1996

> I had such a hard time saying 'see ya' not 'good-bye.' I enjoyed Natalie's sweet disposition. When she started crying, I was so upset. I started crying, too.

On the same day, I mailed Michael a letter, which shared my heart.

June 10, 1996

Michael,

Well, I've been home one day, and it's been one of the hardest days ever. The Lord and I have spent a lot of time together. I need him more than ever. I never dreamed it would be so hard—I'm experiencing too much change too fast. The Lord is my Rock, and I'm ever thankful, because I feel as though all of my other stability has been yanked out from under me. I miss you so much already. Everything reminds me of you, and this drives me crazy. I'm counting down the days 'til I see you again. I feel so cheesy. I've never felt this way before, and maybe I shouldn't be telling you. I don't even know anymore. I rejoice in knowing that God knows! Well, I could write you a book and tell you all about my day, but I won't. Suffice it to say that I'm learning to trust. Thanks for being patient with me as I stumble through this letter. My mind is racing with so many things.

Natalie

Two weeks later, Michael came to visit me. We decided to spend the day together at the beach. On the way, Michael dropped a James Avery brochure between the seats in the car.

"You weren't supposed to see that," he said, grabbing it. A few weeks earlier, Michael had told me about a seashell ring that he had seen at a James Avery store. He had gone on and on about how the ring had reminded him of me. Had he bought that ring for me? Why was he being so secretive?

When we arrived at the beach, we parked my car and strolled down the coast. Coming upon a lifeguard chair, we couldn't resist the urge to climb up in it. We sat on the chair and gazed at the ocean and at each other.

"Hmmm," I sighed unknowingly.

"What is it?" Michael questioned me.

"I was just reminiscing to a time in middle school when I wrote a song about how love is like the ocean." Teasingly, he nudged me, saying, "Well, sing it to me." Slapping at his arm, I playfully responded, "No way!" He wasn't satisfied.

"Well, if you won't sing it to me, then at least tell me the words." I thought for a minute before responding. "Love, love is like the ocean. It has its ups and its downs. I can't do this! I feel so silly," I declared.

Placing my chin in his hand, he lovingly answered, "No it's not. Tell me more." Even though I was afraid to share what was in my heart, I began, "Well, I know love is not about being happy. Love endures the ups and the downs, much like the ocean. When I think of love and marriage, I think of permanence."

Michael reached for my hand and said, "I couldn't agree more. Too many people take marriage lightly. Marriage takes work, but I think it is worth the effort." The conversation had become so intense that neither of us realized that hours had passed while we sat together in the lifeguard chair.

After some time, we climbed down and began walking back to the car. About ten minutes into our stroll, Michael picked up his pace. I was struggling to keep up with him. Before long, he was jogging.

"Slow down," I pleaded. "What's the rush?"

Michael hesitated and finally told me to look at the tide, which had come in considerably. *My car!* If we didn't hurry, it would be mired in sand on the beach! We were both racing back when Michael flagged down a Jeep to help us. We hopped in and sped off toward my car.

As we approached my Bonneville, I gasped. There were ten men surrounding my car, trying to push it out of the ocean. I fell on my knees and began to pray as Michael raced to the car. Anxiously, I watched as he climbed into the car, and my heart swelled with joy as I heard the rumble of the engine as it came to life. Five more minutes and my car would have been washed out to sea!

Tears were streaming down my face as I cried out to the Lord in thanksgiving. At that moment, I was so overcome by the goodness of God that I could not imagine loving him more than I did in that moment. God is my Protector and my Guide, and he loves me deeply. He had blessed my life with an incredible friendship with a man like no other. My heart was so full.

After we washed the undergirding of the car, we went back to the beach for a picnic. (This time, we parked in the lot—not on the beach.) As we ate our sandwiches, we reflected on God's glory. It was truly a time of worship. Finishing up, we decided to take one last stroll before heading back to my parents' house. We kicked off our shoes and headed down the sandy beach. Michael seemed distracted somehow; he kept squeezing his water bottle so that water squirted everywhere. Laughing, I said, "Michael, what is wrong with you? You seem so nervous." He had become unusually quiet.

Finally, Michael grabbed my hand and said, "Come on. I want to show you something." I followed Michael along the sandy path until we found a spot near the dunes to sit down. Michael continued, "I wrote this for you after our last campus ministry meeting at Mercer. I've waited until now to give it to you. I want you to listen."

He read to me:

Natalie,

I have no idea what to say. After this last night of RUF where I thought I was all cried out, I can't help but cry even more right now. But these tears I shed are tears of joy! I'm in the SGA (Student Government Association) office (hence the stationary), and you're outside sharing the love of God with Amy. Natalie, when you told me you were going to share with this girl, I followed you out the door in order to see where you were going and whom you were with. I came to this office to pray. I left this room only to be led to Henry Morris who prayed with me for you. We prayed and I know the Lord is faithful. He used you, I know. He's using you and will use you in the future.

Natalie, Henry disclosed how he feels about us and said he—Natalie, he told me what I already knew but was too scared to say. I need you, Natalie Pope, to be my helpmate, my soul mate, my best friend, my closest sister in Christ. Natalie, I'm in love with the One who brought us together. Oh, but Natalie, there's more— Natalie, I love you! Wow! These words have never been said about you by me until now. But I cannot fight that God is bringing us together anymore. I love every part of you. I'm scared and will not say this to you until I can follow it up with action. I believe God would have us to be married, but I don't know when...

What was happening here? Tears were streaming down my face. Could it be? I began to shake, not believing my ears. Was he—?

I grabbed Michael in a tight embrace. We cried together until, suddenly, Michael jumped up and began slapping sand fleas off his legs. Laughing, he guided me toward the water so that he could rinse off his legs. As the surf rolled over our toes, Michael reached into his pocket and pulled out—*what?* A James Avery bag? He had just told me that he loved me and now he was going to give me a stupid seashell ring?

In what seemed like an eternity, Michael reached inside the velvet bag and pulled out a diamond engagement ring. He dropped to one knee and exclaimed, "Natalie, I love you with all my heart, and I want to spend the rest of my life with you. Will you marry me?

Yes! Yes! A million times—yes! I thought to myself.

He picked me up and spun me around as we both squealed in delight.

"Wait," Michael paused. "You still haven't answered me." Grinning from ear to ear, I yelled, "Yes! Yes, Michael Flake. I will marry you!"

Then it happened—that moment in every girl's dreams. The world seemed to stop as Michael gazed into my eyes, cupped my chin in his hands and ever so gently leaned over and kissed me for the first time.

I know that by today's standards, to have dated without even kissing sounds improbable and maybe even impossible. We both had regrets from past relationships, though, and were dedicated to the idea of saving those precious moments for just one person— the one with whom God designed us to share the rest of our lifetime.

It was worth waiting for!

When our lips finally drew apart, our eyes lifted to the heavens. At that moment, a few days before July 4, fireworks erupted in the sky. Unbelievably, there was also a blue moon.

It was perfect. Our long-awaited first kiss ignited fireworks!

Six whirlwind months later, we were married. Michael had accepted a job working with Georgia Mountain Resort Ministries in North Georgia, and we began our new life together in the mountains. I soon began working with the youth ministry at Helen First Baptist Church.

We were thrilled with our new home. We spent hours there dreaming. The more time we spent at home, the greater the sense grew that there was something missing. We knew that it was time for our family to have a new addition. So we adopted our first little one—a puppy named Gabby!

Our friends, who share our sense of humor, even threw us a shower. I'll never forget Michael cutting a hole into the little diaper and actually putting it on over Gabby's tail. We had a lot of laughs and grew to love our new Labrador.

Every Sunday at church, Michael was responsible for making the morning announcements during worship. He had always been quite the talker, and I never knew what would come out of his mouth. He spoke with contagious enthusiasm and really set the tone for the service as one of anticipation.

As Michael began welcoming everyone to church, he proclaimed, "Natalie and I have been talking and we have decided that our family is incomplete. We agree that it is time for us to have an addition in the Flake family. So, it is with great excitement that I'd like to announce to you…" I cringed inwardly. I couldn't believe he was making such an announcement without discussing it with me first.

Sitting in the choir loft, I was cringing inside. People began leaning over and patting me on the back, wishing me congratulations. I was mortified. Michael finally proceeded to tell everyone about Gabby.

"Yesterday, we adopted our first puppy!" Everyone had a good laugh!

Michael seldom went anywhere without his precious puppy. They went to the river together, fishing together—everywhere. When it became evident that we needed a second vehicle, Michael desperately wanted a truck so Gabby could ride with him. We began to pray and seek the Lord, asking him to help us find one that we could afford. We had very little money in those days, and the idea of a truck payment was overwhelming. A good friend called us one day and told us that he had a Ford Ranger for sale if we were interested.

We drove down to meet him so we could see the truck. As we took the truck for a spin, it didn't take long for me to realize that Michael loved it! Trying to calm himself, Michael suggested that we pray together in the truck and ask God for guidance. We prayed and both felt a peace that this was the truck for us. The only question was whether or not our friend would be willing to work out a payment plan with us.

When we brought the truck back, our friend asked us what we thought about it. Michael said, "Man, I love it! It's great! I only have one question. Will you work with us on a payment plan?"

"Nope," our friend replied. My heart sank. We didn't have any money to pay for the truck up front. Before we could reply, he continued, "My wife and I have prayed about this, and we wanted to make sure that you and Natalie liked the truck. If you like it, we will sell it to you for one dollar!"

We were stunned!

"No way! Are you for real?" Michael shouted, as I stood next to him, speechless, with tears streaming down my face. Our friend and his family grinned as they handed us the keys to our new Ford Ranger.

Michael dug into his wallet and proudly pulled out a crisp one-dollar bill.

We were both so overwhelmed by God's goodness. It seemed like God was pouring out blessings from heaven into every area of our lives. Both the resort ministry and the youth ministry were expanding.

In the midst of all of God's favor, our love for each other deepened. Our marriage was an extended honeymoon. Our first anniversary came and went, but I'll never forget the gift Michael gave to me—a James Avery seashell ring.

The more time that passed, the more madly in love with each other we became. God was so good to us!

Life with Michael was always adventurous. But I had no idea that our romantic comedy was about to become a tragedy.

CHAPTER 3

Because Michael had been such a joyful person, I was shocked when he became severely depressed. More and more frequently, he felt down and discouraged. There was little in life that made him smile. Nothing I did seemed to help, and I began to worry about him. Michael, too, was aware of the change.

Michael always thrived on being around people, but something had changed inside him. One afternoon, I walked into the living room where Michael was sitting in the recliner watching television.

"Michael, Jim and Angie have invited us over for dinner tonight."

He responded, "You go ahead without me. I don't feel like going anywhere."

Frustrated, I urged him, "But, Michael, you haven't been anywhere in days. You sleep and watch TV. It would do you good to get out of the house for a while." I was surprised by his answer.

"No one wants to be around me. I don't really have any friends. Why would anyone want to be my friend? I'm a screw-up! No, I think I'll just stay here." I was astounded! Michael, the man everyone loved, felt all alone, and nothing I tried seemed to help.

On March 18, 2000, he wrote in his journal:

> I shared with Natalie some of my fears. We had
> a great devotion on phantoms. I often feel like
> I have to have everything together all the time.

This causes me to be uptight, and I often shy away from people because I know that I am so unraveled. I am scared of questions that I cannot answer. I am overcome by fear of the unknown. My faith exercised seems so weak and frail. I often cannot bear the responsibility alone. These words seem so vague and nebulous. I really need to seek the counsel of the Holy Spirit. Do not stop your long suffering with me. God, you have been so good to me, and I seem to have such a short-term memory. Please increase my ability to memorize your Word. I want to know you and the power of the resurrection. I want to be a part of the reconciliation movement of God.

I hate phantoms. They seem to paralyze me, and I cannot seem to break free of their elusive control. Lord, I desire to hear from you more than anything else in the world. Oh Lord, can I hear from you? Speak to me through your Word! Make it clear to me. Help me to see where you are the Creator God, Creator of all good things, even of Natalie and me.

Michael continued to lead the resort ministry, but things were different. He was no longer the enthusiastic, carefree man so many had grown to love. Each day after work, he would come home and sit in front of the television for hours. Returning phone calls or carrying on a conversation became burdensome to him. He had always been active and vocal, so this was unusual for him.

"I feel so empty, so alone," he would often tell me. "I feel like I am drowning in an abyss and there's no way to escape. Nothing I do is good enough. No matter how hard I try, I can't seem to shake the sadness."

It hurt my heart to hear such words from a man I loved so dearly. People would tell him to "snap out of it," but that just wasn't possible. It seemed like Michael's downward spiral would never stop. No matter what we tried, he continued to decline.

After a couple of months of feeling this way, Michael finally went to our family doctor, who prescribed an antidepressant. Still, the depression continued to linger, taking Michael down a path of despair. He had little energy, and his attitude was despondent. I had no idea how to help him.

Michael always loved the outdoors. He would jump at the chance to go camping or hiking. His best friend, Chad, called and left a message on the voicemail inviting Michael to go hiking. Even this was not enough to motivate Michael to leave the recliner. No matter how much I pushed, he refused to even return Chad's call.

"It's just too much effort to talk to anyone right now," he said.

"But Michael, this is Chad we are talking about. You love to go hiking with him. Why don't you give him a call?" I suggested. He continued to rest in the recliner, making no move for the phone.

He was so embarrassed. He didn't want anyone to know about the depression. I felt helpless and didn't know where to turn. It seemed that our lives had turned toward a downward spiral. The fact that he didn't want anyone to know about his struggle left me feeling very alone. I didn't feel like I could share my concerns with anyone else, so I kept my own private anxieties to myself.

One sleepless night, Michael wrote:

> I feel so depressed. I don't believe I've ever felt as down in the dumps as I've felt for the past two and a half months. Oh, Lord, if only I could hear from you, and if only you would show me your plan for my life. What I am putting Natalie through is not fair in the slightest. I seem to be forgetting so much of the things that used to make me the happiest. As I pen this entry, I am sitting next to a beautiful waterfall in the Chattahoochee National Forest. My thoughts seem to be colliding into one another. Oh Lord, if only I could have one clear thought and even act out upon it. I would be so much better off.

We felt like we were falling deeper and deeper into a cavern, and we didn't know how to stop. Michael wanted to spend most of his days in bed but forced himself to get up and go to work. When the summer missionaries arrived to work with the ministry, it took everything Michael had to supervise them. In the past, Michael found great delight in getting to know the staff. But this year, it was like everything else—incapable of bringing him out of the pit.

The summer missionaries had never met the vivacious, full-of-life man I fell in love with! They only knew a man who appeared wounded and scattered. Some began voicing their concerns with me.

"Is Michael OK? We don't really see as much of him as we thought we would." I really didn't know how to respond because I didn't want to betray Michael's trust. It was so important to him that he maintain his image of having it all together that he didn't want anyone to know about the depression. Usually, I'd answer the missionaries and others with "He's just not feeling very well."

Summers were always insanely busy for us. Not only did the resort ministry race full speed ahead, but it was also the time of year for me to take the youth at church to camp. As the time for me to leave for camp drew near, Michael became more and more apprehensive about being alone.

"Do you have to go?" he asked.

Uncertain what to do, I replied, "Do you want me to stay home?"

Scratching his head, and shifting his weight he replied, "No. You need to do your job. Go ahead."

We'd been apart on numerous occasions. Where was this insecurity coming from? As I continued to pack, I noticed the tears. "Michael, are you sure you will be OK with me gone?"

He wiped away the tears with the back of his hand. "Yeah, I'm sorry. I'll be fine."

I didn't know what to think or do. I felt pulled between my role as a wife and as a minister.

The day I left, Michael was a complete wreck. He had dark circles under his eyes and hadn't showered in several days. He moped around aimlessly and wept continually. I felt trapped between my responsibility to the church and my devotion to my husband. I decided to be dutiful in my job, so I hit the road camp-bound. As I got closer and closer to our destination, fear began to overtake me. I'd never seen Michael so depressed and so hopeless.

"Don't go, Natalie. I can't bear the thought of being alone. I feel so scared," Michael had said. "I don't know what I am doing anymore. I feel like I am drowning, and I wish you didn't have to go."

"Lord, am I doing the right thing?" I asked.

When I arrived at the conference center, I saw my friend Doug Couch and immediately began to cry. Placing his hand on my shoulder, Doug asked, "Natalie, are you ok?" As much as I tried to hold it in, the tears fell.

"Not really. I'm worried about Michael. He's going through a rough time, and I'm not sure if I should be here at camp or at home with him. He's very depressed and I have to admit I'm scared for him."

Frowning, Doug asked me, "Do you think Michael might hurt himself?" I hadn't really thought about it. Now I really was afraid. Honestly, I didn't know what to expect. Reluctantly I answered, "I really don't know."

Doug reached out and hugged me saying, "Natalie, go home to Michael. We can take care of things here."

When I got to town, I called Michael.

"Michael, I'm at the youth center at church. Can you meet me?" I heard a pause on the line.

"The youth center?" he began. Between tears, Michael said, "I can't believe you came back. I'll be there in ten minutes."

When Michael walked in the door, we raced into each other's arms. We clung to each other like our very lives depended on that moment. When Michael was able to regain his composure to speak, he asked, "Why did you come back?" Looking at him through the tears, I said, "I had to come back. Michael, I am worried about you. I think we need to get some help." He agreed. "You're right. I can't continue to live like this."

It took a few weeks to get an appointment with the doctor, and things continued to worsen with each day. Never before had I been so scared and felt so out of control. I wrote in my journal:

> Dark, dismal days. I've never been so afraid in all my life. Michael has been struggling with anxiety and depression for the last six months. I can't remember the last time he slept through the night. Tonight, he took not only Sonata, but also two Tylenol PM. He's very groggy, and his vision is doubled. He mutters to me. I'm not sure whether this is just giving him rest or if he needs to go to the hospital. Did he take too much? Has he overdosed? What should I do? This is such a lonely place to be.
>
> Lord, grant me wisdom. I know this spirit of fear is not from you. Give me peace. Heal Michael. Lead us to the right counselor. Give him rest, physically and emotionally.
>
> Lord, without you, I'd lose my mind. I hate pretending all is fine when inside I am crumbling. At times I feel I must even hide from Michael so that I can be strong for him but so often my tears give me away. I love him

as I've never loved before, and the thought of losing him tears me apart. Father, please heal my love. Give us the comfort that only comes from above.

Thank you for ministering to my soul in worship last night. Thank you for assuring me of your constant presence. You will never leave me nor forsake me. Be real to Michael. O Healer, free his pain. Help me to be a support to him. Take away my moments of weakness when I want to lash out. May I scream at the sickness and not at you or Michael.

Even though I don't understand at all, thank you. I sing of how I long for brokenness and you have answered that prayer. For so long, I believed that I had to be strong, but no—when I am weak, you are strong. I am right where you want me. Teach me to be content. I love you, Lord!

As I cried out to the Lord, he brought momentary peace to my heart.

A month later, Michael's mood dramatically improved. His joyous spirit was restored, as well as his zest for life. We were ecstatic about the changes in him. We were so happy that the depression was gone and that our lives could return to normal. I can't express how relieved I was to have my husband back! I was so glad that the depression had disappeared.

Unfortunately, our joy was short-lived. Just as things were beginning to look up, things became topsy-turvy. Michael was no longer depressed, nor was he acting like himself. He was easily agitated, manipulative, controlling and, at times, downright mean. This wasn't the man I married. I didn't even like this man. I wrote in my journal:

> I'll never forget sitting in Henry's office in his home for our premarital counseling. One of the questions he asked us will stay with me always. He asked Michael and me why we loved each other. We began to list all of the reasons why. He then asked if we woke up one morning and everything we loved about the other was gone, would we still love them one another? That day, I quickly answered, "Yes!" (without fully knowing the implications). Even today, I am just beginning to understand.
>
> The last six months have been the hardest of my life. Michael's depression was controlling our lives. At times, he was even suicidal. I never knew from one moment to the next who my husband would be. After months of praying for deliverance, we finally sought medical help. Our doctor diagnosed Michael with GAD (General Anxiety Disorder) and put him on medication. After a month without change, the dosage was increased and almost immediately Michael became an obnoxious beast. Who was this man in my husband's body? Surely, he isn't the same man I married.
>
> When the depression subsided, super-hyperactivity set in. Michael still didn't sleep, no longer due to nightmares but now due to excessive energy levels. As he went without sleep, he constantly kept waking me up deeming that six hours of rest was laziness and that I needed

to get up. Without notice, he removed himself from his meds, throwing him into an abyss of hatred and rudeness. Never had I seen Michael behave so poorly, both to me and others. I found myself constantly embarrassed and often apologizing for him. The tears seemed to fall endlessly. Even now, my heart aches.

I didn't want Michael in the pit of despair, but I didn't like his new, out-of-control personality, either. I felt like a yo-yo, being bounced up and down with his ever-changing moods. The worst part was that Michael didn't see it.

"I feel better than I have in years. I don't know why everyone wants me to go back to the doctor." Trying to get him to understand that he was not well was so frustrating.

"But Michael, you are not well. You run around like a chicken with your head cut off and accomplish very little. You're always on edge, and it's driving everyone else crazy." No matter what I said, he couldn't understand.

For months, Michael and I had been planning a vacation in Ellijay. We were both excited about the trip because we needed a break from the craziness of summer. Since the depression had lifted, Michael was convinced that all was well. But it wasn't. As it got closer to time for our vacation, Michael became busier and busier. The summer staff had all gone home, and things were winding down with the resort ministry, but it was as if someone had wound Michael up like a top and set him loose.

Before the sun would rise, Michael would leave for work. We were still sharing an office at the church, and I would come in to find the office a disaster after just having cleaned it the day before. We would put in our hours and I'd go home, but Michael always found more to do. It was amazing, because he was so busy—yet he was accomplishing so little. He would often stay at work until after midnight. He would call me all day long and want me to join him on some excursion.

"Natalie, what are you doing? Let's go to the park and have a picnic," he'd say. Two hours later, he would call again.

"Natalie, it's gorgeous outside. What do you say we go for a walk?" As nice as a walk might have been, I had work to do, and so did he.

"Michael, I can't. I'm working." Before I could even refocus, the phone would ring again.

"If you don't want to go for a walk, how about we go visiting? There are lots of people we haven't seen lately." Michael seemed to have lost all concept of time, and work was no longer a priority. Three days passed without Michael taking a shower, and he called our friends and bragged about this. He was proud because he had so much energy.

Finally, it was the day for our departure. I had packed all our bags so we could leave that morning. I awoke to find a note that said, "Be back shortly." I got dressed, loaded the car, and waited for Michael to return. I waited. And waited. And waited. No Michael. At noon, I began to call him. After several tries, I finally reached him on the phone. He was ecstatic.

"Natalie, you'll never believe what I found out!" he gushed. "Ground school is going on this week. I called and I can take classes toward my solo pilot's license!"

"What about our vacation?" I questioned.

He exclaimed, "We're still going. I'll just drive to Atlanta every afternoon for class and I'll be back at night. We'll have the mornings together."

Needless to say, I was in quite a tizzy. I had been looking forward to this trip for months. Surely he wouldn't leave me on vacation in the mountains alone.

Would he?

We drove to Ellijay and unpacked. The whole time, I was hoping that he'd given up on the whole flight school idea. After dinner, I put in a movie by Gary Smalley about marriage, when Michael announced, "Good. I'm really glad you chose that one. Enjoy it while I'm gone."

He was seriously going to flight school! This vacation was about us, and he wanted me to work on our marriage alone while he drove all the way to Atlanta and back.

I was livid. After he left, I wept like never before. The tears seemed endless. What was becoming of our marriage? We had always been so close—best friends. I didn't even know who Michael was anymore. I was afraid. Would the man I knew and loved ever be the same again?

Michael didn't see anything wrong with the arrangement. He left about 3:30 each afternoon and drove to Atlanta, returning about 11:00 each night. He woke up early every morning to study his lessons for flight school. We'd go to the river or the pool for a couple of hours and then he was off again!

I did a lot of thinking in those lonely hours. My prayer was for the Lord to daily increase my commitment to Michael and allow me to cherish our vows. It was not an easy prayer, but I was sincere and kept praying it. Somehow, we survived the week and returned home.

This cycle of desperate highs and lows continued. Our doctor suggested that Michael see a therapist, so we began meeting with a Christian counselor who gave us many practical suggestions to help with the depression. Still, while the counselor was helping, it wasn't enough.

We eventually began to look for a psychiatrist. Entering this new territory was terrifying, but the results were astounding. The doctor explained to us that Michael was experiencing a mild form of mania. He explained that this often caused hyperactivity and increased anxiety. He prescribed a new regimen of drugs and things slowly began to improve.

Michael became much more amiable. With the help of our counselor, we were finally able to talk through some of our issues. Healing had begun in both of our lives and in our marriage.

Still dreaming of serving together on the international mission field, we moved to Louisville, KY, to attend seminary. The day before we left North Georgia, we found out that we were having a baby. I was ecstatic! Surely our lives were turning around. Michael was doing well. We were pursuing our dreams, and now we were expanding our family!

As classes began, I found myself absolutely in love with the academic community. Michael, on the other hand, was miserable. He was having a difficult time making friends, and he had become anti-social—totally different from the man I'd married.

There were days when I couldn't get Michael out of bed to go to class. This was especially challenging because we had all our classes together. The professors would always ask me where Michael was, and I didn't know how to answer. How do you tell them, "He didn't come to class because he's feeling sorry for himself, and he's really down?" Instead, I'd give the standard, "He's not feeling so good."

There were other days when Michael would cry for hours. This was a difficult time for us. I was pregnant, which meant both Michael and I were on a roller coaster ride of emotions. I felt like I was always trying to pull him up.

We started seeing another counselor, and he looked Michael squarely in the eye, and said, "Your erratic behavior patterns appear to be attributed to your bipolar disorder." Michael's jaw dropped.

"What? I don't have bipolar disorder," Michael demanded. "No one has ever told me this before. Where did you get such a crazy notion?" Michael retorted.

The doctor continued, "Michael, I'm sorry no one has ever told you, but it is in your records. You need to acknowledge that you have a mental illness. You have bipolar disorder." This news devastated Michael. He denied the possibility for weeks.

"Natalie, you don't believe what the doctor said, do you? Tell me you don't think I'm crazy," he would plead. I'd answer as calmly as I could muster.

"No, Michael, I don't think you are crazy, but we have to admit that you haven't been yourself for some time now. Maybe we should consider the possibility that the doctor is right." He was embarrassed and ashamed. As I researched the disorder, I became convinced that this could be a legitimate diagnosis.

As we progressed in our schoolwork, Michael's misery deepened.

We realized that it would be very difficult for both of us to continue to go to school once we had our baby. We began to pray and seek the Lord. Despair seemed to define Michael during those days. He hated the cold, snowy days. He hated the city life. He longed for the mountains. He began to dream of moving back to Cleveland to start our family.

I had my doubts. The church had sent us off to seminary with the understanding that we'd become international missionaries. What would everyone think if we packed up and came home after one semester?

When our pastor called, Michael shared his desire to return. I was pleasantly surprised when Pastor Jim assured Michael saying, "We love you. I know that the church would welcome you back with open arms. You are going through a difficult time, and you need support. Let us be that support for you." His encouragement was a relief and answer to prayer. We returned to Georgia and Michael resumed the same job he had left behind.

I wish I could say that everything got better. In fact, it got worse.

About a month after we got back, Georgia Mountain Resort Ministries hosted a carnival downtown. By then, I was eight months pregnant. Since I couldn't stand the scorching heat for very long, I worked at the hospitality center for our volunteers. Michael showed up late in the afternoon and asked, "Hey, will you ride with me to the church to pick up some more balloon animals and water bottles?"

Reluctantly, I agreed. "Ok, I'll go."

All the way to the church, Michael berated me.

"You don't care about my ministry, do you? Why did you even come? Why aren't you outside working?"

I tried to explain. "Michael, I'm eight months pregnant and it's ninety degrees outside. I'm working at the hospitality room inside." He wasn't satisfied.

He yelled, "Well, the least you could have done was bring me something cold to drink while you sit inside enjoying the air conditioner, knowing your husband is dying of heat. And what about lunch? You didn't bring me any lunch, either!"

On and on he went. By the time we got to the church, I was furious. I lit into him.

"Michael, that's enough! I'm sick and tired of you yelling at me. You are mean and manipulative. You need to change your attitude or you're going to end up running this carnival alone. Do you know how many people have come into the hospitality center complaining about your behavior?" Maybe it was not the right way to respond, but I was furious.

He looked at me with hatred in his eyes, and said, "You are a sorry excuse for a wife. If you cared about me at all, then you would be outside working beside me all day. I don't know why I put up with you!"

He began cussing at me and I looked at him and said, "I'm not going to take this. I'm leaving." As I turned to walk out of the church, he grabbed me and threw me over his shoulder. I began kicking and screaming.

"Put me down! You're going to hurt the baby! Stop it! Quit!" On and on, I pleaded with him to put me down. I was terrified. I was so afraid that he was going to hurt the baby. I thought about yelling for help, but no one else was in the church.

I'm not sure what got through to him, but he finally threw me off his shoulder and sat me in a chair, where he held his hands firmly on my shoulders, making sure I couldn't go anywhere. He got right in my face and began to cry.

"I am so sorry," he said. "I should have never done that. I'm hot, I'm tired, and I've got to get back to work. We'll talk more later." That was the end of the discussion. He drove me back to the concessions area where I stayed the remainder of the day with a lot on my mind.

How dare he treat me that way! How could the gracious, compassionate, loving man I married have turned into such a monster? I wrestled with this question and more in the weeks that followed.

By the time August rolled around, the medication had finally taken effect, and Michael's mood began to stabilize. We both began to prepare for the birth of our precious little girl with eager anticipation.

On August 28, 2001, Rebekah Jorjanne Frances Flake was born. Michael was so supportive that day. He was thrilled to be a new dad! We both thanked God for blessing us with the joy of a little one.

The first couple of months after we brought our daughter home were special. Michael and I grew closer as we discovered the joys of parenting. We would stand beside Jorjanne's bed and watch her sleep. Michael would lie in the floor beside her and try and make her smile. We floated in a continuous state of awe that God had given us such a precious gift.

Unfortunately, that was just the calm before the next storm. We continued to walk through an abyss of highs and lows. In the beginning of his illness, Michael was depressed about twice a year. As time passed, he became depressed three to four times a year and was manic just as often. At long last, the psychiatrist confirmed what we had suspected for a while—he had bipolar disorder.

Now that we knew what was plaguing Michael, we hoped that he would find some relief from its horrors. As he began to accept this diagnosis, he journaled:

April 17, 2003

Well, it all seems to boil down to the quality of life issue. Do I want to continue on with the massive cycles from extreme highs to extreme lows? I am going through the wringer of emotions again. Kathy [our counselor] says that I am chronic. I have a chronic disease. I am bipolar. If it had been forty years ago, I'd be in and out of hospitals, but now I have medicine, and for me not to take it means I'm throwing away the gift God is giving me. I really need to get more focused and stay focused. Lord, please help me. My thoughts run as rapid as the stream behind me here at Panther Creek. If only they could run in the same direction as the stream and not everywhere. I've got to leave this place and get some work done. Oh Lord, where is my passion for life? Where is it? Help me, Lord, to trust in you. My words seem so meaningless right now. Please put meaning back in my words, Oh Lord!

What words can I put on this page or on any page that could really express the total sadness in my heart? I have lost my passion for life and for living. Constantly I struggle with sad thoughts and feelings of hopelessness. Where, O God, are you? Where is the passion I once had? Am I just living a life of confusion? I lack the clarity of thought to make wise decisions. What is it that clogs my ears so I cannot even hear your still, small voice? Why, O God, must I suffer with this living hell? Where are you when I call out to you?

O God, surely there is more to life. I feel like such a hypocrite. Why do I have no joy and a cloud of doubt that hangs heavy around my spirit? Where are you in my life? Why is this my lot? Oh God, please free me from this awful depression! I feel safest in bed all curled up. Why are my thoughts so jumbled? Why must Natalie endure this again? Where is my positive attitude and my joy for living? Where are you, oh Lord? Why am I so dead?

Eventually, Michael went back to the doctor, and his medications were adjusted again. Michael was still having a hard time accepting that he needed medications.

Michael told me, "Natalie, I keep hearing voices in my head telling me that the doctor doesn't really care about me. If he did, he wouldn't charge such exorbitant fees." Michael knew these voices were lying to him, but he still heard them and, at times, he listened. Taking medicine was a constant battle for Michael. Once again, he abandoned his medication, and the depression returned.

Each time Michael would stop taking his medication, I would become infuriated with him! Why couldn't he just take the stupid medicine? After all, it was helping him. Every time he came off of the meds, he put us back on the roller coaster. I was at the end of my rope and didn't know where to turn for help. In desperation, I wrote:

> My heart hurts like never before. My daughter looks at me with compassion and says, "Are you sad, Mommy?" How should I respond? I'm dying! My husband treats me like a slave—if I question him or fail to do his every wish I am told I no longer care about our marriage. I was yelled at for throwing away the packaging for chicken, cool whip, and strawberries. He yells at me for cleaning; he yells because I don't clean. Lord, what am I to do? I'm in a no-win situation. There is no peace in my life right now.

I'm living in turmoil. Please help his medicine to work! I can't continue to live like this.

What am I to do? I am committed to this marriage, but I refuse to be treated with such continual disrespect. Should Jorjanne and I leave for a while? If so, where do we go? She needs stability and consistency, and I can't provide either when Michael is so unpredictable.

Earlier this week, Michael hung my pajamas all over the house and put his clothes in my drawer. When I asked him about this, he walked around, grabbing my pajamas from the house, and began throwing them into the trash. I tried to talk with him, but he refused to listen. To my knowledge—my pajamas are gone, much like my dignity.

My love language is quality time, but that is impossible right now. When I have time alone with Michael, he tells me all I am doing wrong and that I don't care. I am standing beside him because I do care! Father, I don't know what to do or not to do. Perhaps the hardest thing is knowing we may have this "thorn" for the rest of our lives.

Draw Michael unto yourself. Make him a man after your own heart. Help him to see his mania. Give him the desire to change. Protect Jorjanne. Guard her eyes from this. Help her not to see her daddy in a bad light. Help me to trust. Lord, be my strength, my Rock, and my Fortress. I need the comfort found in the safety of your arms. Hold me and give me peace.

Michael's mania continued to escalate. He spent several nights at the office because he had "so much work to do." He'd come home and shower—on a good day—and then leave again. From what I could tell, he wasn't accomplishing much in his hours at work. People began calling our house looking for him because he had failed to return their phone calls. I made excuses for him and tried to cover as best I could. I cried every day for two months. I feared I'd never smile again.

Summer was quickly approaching, and numerous volunteers would soon be coming to North Georgia, and Michael was responsible for scheduling their assignments. He asked me to help him make out a schedule for the summer. Before I could get out of bed, he left with Jorjanne to go hiking, so I got up and worked on some schoolwork.

He came home and began shouting, "Why aren't you working on the schedule? I thought we agreed when I left to work on the schedule?"

Shocked, I shouted back. "Michael, you've been hiking. You didn't seriously expect me to do your job for you while you were out playing, did you? We can work on it together now that you are home."

Michael responded by yelling, "You don't care about me or my job. I don't need your help!" He stormed out of the house and began working in the yard.

After some time, I cautiously approached him and asked, "Do you want to work in the yard or do you want my help with scheduling?" I should have stayed out of his way.

"I told you I don't need your help! You don't care about me, so just leave me alone!" he screamed.

Jorjanne and I loaded into the van to get away for a while. I just needed some space. I was putting the car in reverse when he picked up the doghouse and set it behind the van so I couldn't leave. He climbed into the backseat of the van and proceeded to yell at me. After much shouting from both of us, Jorjanne looked at Michael and said, "Daddy, get out of this car and go."

Oh, how my heart broke! Our little girl was seeing all of this! What had become of us? Michael angrily burst out of the car, and I drove to a friend's house so I could clear my head. Several hours later, we returned home to find Michael asleep in the backyard.

I felt like the pain would never end. Every winter, Michael sank into the abyss. In the summer, he soared into space. When would it end? Again, I poured out my heart in my journal:

May 9, 2004

Lord, you know what has happened, and you know what it will take to bring healing. I hurt like I've never hurt in my life. I keep thinking there are no more tears to cry, but here they come again. Will they ever stop? Will I know happiness again this side of heaven? I need to be strong for Jorjanne's sake. She needs stability, and nothing seems stable in our home anymore. Life is chaotic. Give me the peace that surpasses understanding.

I know your plans are greater than what we can imagine; help me to live in light of this truth. I can't carry this burden alone. First and foremost, I need you. Secondly, I need the Body of Christ to help strengthen me each day. I've never felt so alone in all my life. I'm desperate for you, Lord! Please carry me through!

A month passed, but the mania did not. Michael and I went to a counseling session, where we talked about finances. Michael had been on several spending sprees, and money was tight. The session went well, and we ventured to Walmart afterward to pick up a few necessities. As we were walking inside, Michael said, "We are going to buy a tree together today and plant it as a reminder of this day as a financial milestone in our marriage." He began to point out all the different trees, asking me if I liked any of them. I was so frustrated because we'd just spent an hour talking with a counselor about how little money we had.

Finally I spoke up and said, "Michael, I don't want a plant. We need to save our money." I turned and began to walk off when he hollered, "Natalie, stop! Come here. Don't walk ahead of me." He was treating me like a child. I bit my tongue and turned and walked back to him. He picked up a twenty-dollar Christmas tree and put it into the buggy.

I said to him, "I really don't think we need another tree."

That did it! He lit into me and began swearing at me. Never before had I heard such talk come out of his mouth. A lady looking at plants nearby glanced our way and began backing away. I said, "Michael, I'll wait for you in the car." He followed me to the car and berated me all the way.

"You are so selfish! It's always about you. I want to buy a tree to symbolize the new life for our marriage, but no, you don't care. You never care!"

I clammed up and then he screamed and cussed because I wasn't talking to him. Embarrassed and angry, I mumbled back, "Michael, I can't talk to you when you are like this."

He yelled, "You never talk to me! You don't care about our marriage." His words hurt more than he would ever know. It was love—not the emotion, but the verb—that kept us together.

Later that night, I wrote in my journal:

> Lord, I know he is unwell, and I know we are all sinners. How do I respond? I'm so tired of this mess. It would be so easy to just give up. Do I get some space between us for a while? Do I allow myself to be spoken to with such disdain and disrespect? Help me, Lord. I want to show Christ's *agape* love to him but it's so hard. I never dreamed I'd be in a marriage where I was treated like trash. He even told me, "I wouldn't treat you like a dog if you didn't act like one." Ouch!
>
> Father, I know our marriage isn't pleasing to you. It must either disgust you or break your heart. Heal our marriage. Heal our hurts. Help me to be a woman pleasing to you. Hold my tongue. Help me to watch Michael fall if that's what it takes and help me to do so without nagging him. Help!

As time progressed, so did Michael's mental illness. I could no longer cover for him at work. His attitude with his staff was unacceptable, and his supervisors called him in for a meeting. When asked how he was doing, Michael readily admitted that things had gotten off to a rocky start. His supervisors told him that he needed to get help and that they were granting him a leave of absence from work. He would be out of work for the duration of the summer.

Reluctantly, Michael agreed to visit the psychiatrist—mainly to appease his employers. A few days later, we met with the psychiatrist, and Michael was visibly antsy. He had a difficult time sitting still, and his thoughts were bouncing from topic to topic.

The doctor asked Michael, "Have you had any thoughts of hurting yourself in the past?"

"Yes," Michael answered.

"Have you had any of those thoughts recently?" the doctor continued.

Michael paused, looked at the floor and whispered, "Yes, I have." The doctor explained to Michael that he needed to go to a hospital.

"At the hospital, you will receive better treatment. They will be able to monitor your medications and help you get the disorder under control. What do you think?" There was a long silence. Finally Michael mumbled, "OK."

The doctor offered to call an ambulance, but without really thinking about it, I said, "I'll drive him."

His nerves really got the best of him as we drove to the hospital.

"Natalie, I am so scared. I don't really need any more help. I'll be ok. Let's just go home," he pleaded. "I promise I will take my medications and everything will be better." I wished that somehow I could believe him, but I knew that if I didn't take him to the hospital now, he would never go.

"Michael, the doctor thinks the hospital is the best place for you now. We need to go." My head ached and so did my heart as he begged me not to go.

"Please, please. I am begging you, Natalie. Don't make me go there. I'll do anything. Just please don't make me go to the hospital."

As we pulled into the parking lot, Michael began vomiting. He was more nervous than I'd ever seen him. He sat in the car and refused to get out. He began to sob uncontrollably. I kept coaxing him and pleading with him, and after thirty minutes in the parking lot, he reluctantly agreed to go inside with me.

Once inside, Michael was escorted into a separate room for a psychological evaluation. I sat in the waiting room, praying that this would help him. After what seemed like forever, a staff member came and took me into the room with Michael.

"Mrs. Flake, the doctor signed a 10-13, which means that Michael has to stay here until a psychiatrist releases him." I glanced over at Michael, and he was livid. He sat with his arms crossed and gritted his teeth. He shot daggers at me with his eyes.

As soon as the counselor left the room, he lit into me.

"You knew it! You don't care about me! You just want me locked up and out of your life. You and the doctor conspired against me!" After a cascade of accusations, he told me to leave.

"Go! Get out of here! I don't want you here, and I don't care if I ever see you again! You are a liar. You and the doctor connived and planned a way to lock me away. I hate you!" I fell into a chair and began to sob.

"Michael, that's not true. I love you. I just want you to get help. Your job is on the line. You desperately need help. We need help!" I cried.

He gave me the silent treatment. He refused to even look at me while I sat with him for another half hour in total silence.

The intake specialist returned and said to Michael, "It's time to take you to your room. Mrs. Flake, you are welcome to walk with us so you can see where Michael will be staying." We walked down a long, cold hallway, through multiple locked doors, and finally entered the wing where Michael would stay.

The first person we saw was a man in his mid-twenties who had suffered a head injury and had wires coming out of his head. The next man who walked by was mumbling obscenities under his breath.

Michael turned to me and pleaded, "Please don't leave me here." My heart was breaking. We were given a tour of the ward and then we had a few minutes alone before I had to leave. Michael began crying, begging me not to leave him in this place. Walking away from him in that moment was one of the hardest things I have ever done.

As the escort unlocked the door and closed it behind us, I was startled by a loud thump. I turned to see a man being wrestled to the ground and put in restraints.

Trembling, I asked, "What just happened?"

The specialist explained, "The man you saw was trying to escape. They will sedate him and put him in isolation for the disturbance."

I fell apart before I even made it to my car. I cried until there were no more tears to cry. Would Michael be okay here? Did we do the right thing? My heart was aching, and I was so fearful for him. Broken and weak, I drove myself home to take care of our daughter.

When Sunday rolled around, I knew that I needed to go to church, but I wasn't sure if I could handle it, so I did what every "good" Christian does. I put on a good front and I went. I smiled on the outside, while inside I was crumbling. Two friends knew what was going on, as did our pastor. I could hardly look them in the eye for fear that I would start crying. I sat in the back, and as soon as the service ended, I darted out the door.

I talked to Michael on the phone every night. The first conversation was heated. Michael was still furious with me for "sending" him to the hospital. In time, the anger subsided, and he began to admit that he had a very real problem. The following weekend was Family Weekend at the hospital. My parents kept Jorjanne so I could go to the hospital and take classes about mental illness. At the workshop, I met other family members who were trying to help their loved ones cope with mental illness.

I came to recognize that I had become co-dependent. I thought by covering up for Michael (returning phone calls for him, answering emails, going to his office after dark) that I was helping him. I learned that I was actually enabling him to continue down a destructive path. I was preventing him from facing the consequences of his actions. I realized that, as hard as it would be to watch him fall, that might be the very thing he needed to help him rise.

I went to some classes by myself and to others with Michael. We attended group therapy and were able to sit down together with the doctor and talk about our own circumstances. This time was beneficial to us as individuals and as a couple. Throughout the weekend, Michael actually came to the realization that he was thankful that he was getting help. He also recognized that he was not "crazy" or "stupid," but that he was a normal guy who had an illness. We met doctors, lawyers, professors, and other professionals who struggled with bipolar disorder. This helped Michael to understand that this illness does not discriminate and helped tear down some of the stigma we carried regarding bipolar disorder. When the weekend was over, I returned home, and a few days later, I was able to go and bring Michael home.

During the time of his hospitalization, I simply told Jorjanne that her daddy was out of town. Anyone who called received the same answer. While we were coming to terms with the illness, we were still not ready to be open about it with others. Michael resumed work in the fall and things improved—for a time.

After a few months of relative calm, the rapid cycling resurfaced. Things got so bad over the holidays while we were visiting my family that Michael returned home without us. My parents were afraid for me, and encouraged me to stay with them until Michael's mania subsided. I had to have a break or I was going to have my own mental breakdown. We spent most of the month of January apart from each other.

During this separation, Michael went to many of our friends and told them that I was leaving him.

"I think Natalie is leaving me. I don't understand why, but she has moved in with her parents."

Friends began calling me, asking, "Why are you leaving Michael? He loves you. You need to come home. Y'all could go to counseling."

They were unaware of Michael's illness. I had no intention of divorcing Michael; I only needed some space before I lost my mind and ended up in a mental health facility myself. I wanted to protect Michael, so I didn't tell most of the people who called about his illness. I tried to explain that things were complicated, and I simply said that I would return home when the time was right.

The more calls that came, the angrier I became at Michael. I felt like he was making me into the bad guy. It was hard enough being away for so long, but it was that much harder when I had to lie about why I was away.

I finally said, "Michael, I am done with the lies. I will not cover for you anymore. I cannot pretend everything is okay when it isn't." I needed his blessing to tell others about his illness.

He did not want me to tell anyone what was going on.

"Natalie, you can't tell anyone. What would they think? I am a minister. I am supposed to have it all together. We can't tell people." He still didn't understand. I tried to explain.

"Michael, I need support. I'm going to lose my sanity if I can't share with one or two people we both trust. I need a safe place to be real." The realization began to dawn on him and he hesitantly agreed.

"OK, you can share with someone, but we both need to agree on who to tell."

At the end of January, Jorjanne and I returned home. Michael was beginning to come down from the mania, and healing had begun once again in our marriage. We continued to go to counseling, and we tried very hard to communicate with each other. Michael had a renewed passion for his ministry and was seeking restoration with many of the people he had hurt. Hope seemed a possibility in our lives.

In early spring, we were hosting a Resort Ministry Conference to train and equip leaders who would be bringing teams to the North Georgia area to work. Michael had invited other resort missionaries from the Southeast to come and speak at the different sessions. Things were advancing well, and I was so proud of Michael. For some reason, he didn't share in my excitement. He was terrified of the conference being a flop. "What am I doing?" he would say. The closer it got to the conference, the more I felt Michael pulling back. His attitude became negative, and his self-confidence all but disappeared.

The day before the conference, Michael told me that he needed some time alone to get ready for the event. He had not been sleeping well for weeks; he had even seen the doctor and gotten a prescription to help him rest. I went to the resort ministry office to work on some final details for the event and was gone all morning. After lunch, I tried to call Michael, but he didn't answer. I assumed he was sleeping. I continued working and about 3:00 p.m. I decided to stop and go work out. As I was driving to the gym, I felt an overwhelming sense of panic. It was as if God told me to go home. I tried to shrug off the feeling, but I kept hearing this pervasive voice in my mind telling me to go home.

Reluctantly, I made a U-turn and went home. I walked in the door and called for Michael. There was no answer. I went into our bedroom and found Michael sleeping soundly. I went over to wake him, but he didn't move. I shook him and called out his name. Still, he didn't move. At first I thought he was playing around with me. I shook him again. Panic threatened to overtake my voice when he didn't respond. Had he taken a sleeping pill? I was furious with him for not waking up.

"Michael, wake up! This is not funny. Get out of bed!"

I walked around the bed, placed both hands on his shoulders, and began to shake him. He didn't respond.

Not sure what to do, I called our friend Jim and told him what was happening.

"Jim, I think I should call 911. What do you think?"

Without hesitating, Jim said, "Yes, make the call."

As I called 911, I walked into the bathroom, searching for clues. I saw the bottle of sleeping pills on the counter and picked it up. *Oh God, no!* The bottle was empty, and it had only been filled a couple of days earlier. I stayed on the phone with the dispatcher while the ambulance was en route. When they got to the house, they gave Michael something to make him throw up the medicine in his system. Before long, he went from being incoherent to vomiting yellow stuff all over our bed. My heart was racing. I began pacing the floor, wondering what in the world I should do. A million thoughts raced through my mind.

Before the EMTs left, Jim was at my house. As we followed the ambulance to the hospital, Jim called Michael's mom and my parents for me. The doctors gave Michael charcoal to help eject the contaminants in his system. Our former pastor and friend, Kyle, and his wife, Alanna, were on their way to the Resort Ministry Conference, so we called and told them what happened. They came to be with me, and I collapsed in Alanna's arms. Kyle waited with us at the hospital as we awaited Michael's prognosis.

I'll never forget Kyle holding a pan for Michael while he vomited charcoal everywhere. It was a disturbing but selfless picture of true friendship.

Eventually, someone from mental health came and evaluated Michael. He told us, "Mr. Flake is going to have to go to a psychiatric hospital tonight." Michael was still nonresponsive.

I asked, "Will you please call his doctor and see if we can get him into the hospital where he went before?" Unfortunately, it had no openings, so Michael was admitted to a local facility.

As we prepared to leave, I realized that the conference was scheduled for the next day. I couldn't possibly deal with the conference tomorrow. There was no way I could face everyone in light of what had just happened. I began to panic.

Kyle lovingly hugged me and said, "I'll take care of tomorrow. You go home and get some rest." All I could think about was what we would tell people about Michael. I couldn't tell them he overdosed. He would be humiliated! What should we do? After much deliberation on my part, I decided that it was best to tell people that he was in the hospital due to a reaction to some medication.

It's the truth, right? I told myself.

It was early in the morning by the time I got home. After a restless night, I got up with an aching in my chest. Because of the conference, Jorjanne was spending the weekend with my parents, so it was a blessing that she had not been home to see any of this. However, the house was deathly quiet that morning, and I hurt.

In the midst of my pain, my dad called me. "Natalie, I'm not sure how to tell you this, but your mom and I talked, and you need to know."

"Know what?" I wondered.

"You see, Natalie, Michael was planning a surprise party for your birthday. He invited all of the family and lots of friends to come to the church tomorrow after the conference and surprise you. We need to get in touch with everyone and cancel the party."

Now I had to cancel my own surprise party? How could I face everyone? I wanted to go away and escape life, but, instead, Michael got to go away, and I was stuck to pick up all the pieces. My sadness quickly turned to anger.

The next day, I went to visit Michael at the hospital. Michael hugged me over and over, saying, "I wasn't trying to take my life, Natalie. You have to believe me. I was just so exhausted that I needed sleep. No matter what I tried, I couldn't rest, so I decided to do whatever it took to get sleep. I took two pills and was still awake. An hour later, I took more. Honestly, I don't remember how many I took." I was skeptical, but I so desperately wanted to believe that he was telling the truth that we never discussed it again.

While I was there, I asked to speak to a doctor. No one at the hospital would talk to me. It was against their regulations to discuss a patient's treatment with family. Michael even asked the doctor to call me, but he refused. Michael had no idea how long he would be there. We both felt helpless.

In the meantime, I called Michael's psychiatrist.

"Michael is in the hospital, and I'd like for him to be transferred to Ridgeview so that he is under your care."

The doctor replied, "As soon as a bed opens up, I will make sure that Michael is moved."

On my birthday, Michael was released from the hospital. He was able to come home that night, but the next morning he was to report to Ridgeview Hospital. We spent the day together in superficial conversation. Neither of us discussed what had occurred. It was almost like we both wanted to pretend it had never happened. It was after all, my thirtieth birthday. It had been hard enough without revisiting it.

The next morning, I drove Michael to the psychiatric hospital where he stayed for several weeks. I went to visit on the weekend for another family workshop, and I was able to meet with his doctor and attend seminars to learn even more about bipolar disorder. Finally, Michael was transferred to the day program, and he spent his days in treatment, but was able to leave at night. We did this for several more weeks. His employers were so gracious to us during this time. He was off work for several months, and they continued to send his paycheck. What a blessing!

While Michael was away, life was tough at home. I was constantly afraid of the phone calls. I found myself making up excuses for why Michael was away. I lived in constant fear of his boss calling to fire him. My house felt as though it was built on sand, and it was shifting day by day. Never had I felt so alone. God was my only strength and refuge.

Five months later, Michael was finally released from the hospital's care. He still had regular doctor visits but no longer had to go to the hospital daily. He seemed more "himself" than he had in years. I felt as though I finally had my husband back. We spent time together;

we played together; he and Jorjanne spent lots of time playing hide and seek, pretending to blast-off, and just plain old wrestling. Life was beginning to look up, and I was cautiously optimistic. After years of searching, I had finally found my husband again. The Lord had restored his joy, and his moods had stabilized.

Michael was learning to recognize the warning signs of his illness and was doing a better job at managing the symptoms. He wrote in his journal:

> These pages are turning faster and faster as the years go by. I feel like I am in a really good place now. I've enjoyed this for about sixteen weeks. I've been looking for triggers and have noticed a few major ones. Additional stress, for one. Not just the kind that comes from daily living but also the kind that comes during the holidays. Forgetting my quiet time with the Lord does not help at all. Thank you, Lord, for helping me.

Now that Michael recognized his triggers, he had to face the challenge of overcoming them.

The first real test came the next day, as we faced the first holiday since his road to recovery had begun. Wednesday morning, we left to celebrate Thanksgiving with family. We found out when we arrived that my aunt had been diagnosed with lung cancer. Everyone was pretty nervous about this—everyone except for Michael.

I was amazed at his ability to calm a stressful situation. He even stayed up late, talking with my aunt, encouraging her to trust the Lord in the midst of the storm. I was so proud of Michael that weekend. This was a crucial moment in my heart. For the first time in years, I was beginning to respect and admire my husband again.

We survived Thanksgiving without a hitch, and I was beginning to remember all the reasons why I fell in love with Michael. It had been four months since he had experienced any bipolar symptoms. We had begun putting the broken pieces of our marriage back together; I found myself truly enjoying my husband's company once again.

A couple of days after Thanksgiving, we took Amtrak cross-country—from Atlanta to Reno—for a conference. We spent a lot of quality time in cramped quarters. We talked and even dreamed together of our future. We watched movies on the train and shared our deepest thoughts with each other. We had a layover in Washington D.C., so we decided to do a little sightseeing. Hand-in-hand, we traversed D.C. We talked about taking Amtrak to D.C. and bringing Jorjanne when she was older. We talked about what it would be like to raise a teenager. We discussed what our lives would look like as we aged and what we would do after retirement. We were both happier than we'd been in a long time; we were falling in love all over again.

We eventually made it to the conference. Reconnecting with old friends was a blessing for both of us. During this time, Michael spent time with a friend named David. David had heard rumors of Michael's mood swings, and so he just asked him straight out what was going on. At first, Michael tried to divert the questions, but eventually, he began to open up. For the first time, Michael was honest about his struggles. He told David about the illness, the medications, his resistance to take the medicines, and his fears. I was so proud of Michael. This was a real break-through for him. He was finally accepting his illness and was beginning to have the courage to face it!

December came into our lives as a sweet kiss on a cold winter morning. Michael dimmed the lights and played Christmas carols on the CD player as the three of us decorated our Christmas tree. Michael put Jorjanne on his shoulders and let her hang ornaments near the top of the tree. Giggling, she clung to his neck. At times, Jorjanne would even lean down and kiss the top of Michael's head. Turning off all the lights, Michael put the angel on the top of the tree. He then offered up a prayer for our family. As he said, "Amen," he turned the lights on the tree so that the moment we opened our eyes, we saw everything glowing and cheerful. It was magical! Michael leaned over and kissed me, assuring me that we had been offered a new start. We were so blessed!

Filled with happiness and joy, I took a group of students from church to Passion (a conference for college students). For the first time in a long while, I was able to worship the Lord with gladness and praise in my heart. God had not only restored my marriage, but also he had restored my joy.

In one of the first sessions, John Piper spoke about the reality of suffering.

"Suffering exists to display the greatness of the glory of God's grace." He continued, "If you are a missionary, you should expect hardship because the only way others see how satisfied we are in Christ is through suffering."

Was that what God had been doing in our lives? I listened to him and prayed that God would use the turmoil of the past four years for His glory—even as I felt relief that the worst was behind me.

Later, as I looked at the list of breakout sessions, one stood out to me. It was entitled, "When Life Hurts," led by Francis Chan. In his talk, Chan spoke about times in his own life when God didn't make sense. As I listened to him share, I felt the weight of all that I had experienced. Still, I was praising God for delivering us from it.

In the midst of my praise, Chan asked the crowd, "How many of you want to be like Jesus?" Hands shot up all over the room; of course we wanted to be like Jesus! Next he asked, "How would you respond if God told you that the only way to make you more like Jesus was to bring suffering into your life?"

Now wait a minute, I thought. *My life has been a living hell, and the last thing I want is to face more suffering.* In that moment, the Holy Spirit spoke to me and said, "But don't you want to be more like Jesus?" Immediately, my heart cried out, "Yes Lord, but—"

I don't remember much else about the session. At that moment, the Lord began carving away at my will. I left the session and kept hearing Chan's question resounding in my mind: "What if the only way for you to become more like Jesus is through suffering?"

I began wrestling with the Lord. "NO! I don't want more suffering! Haven't we had enough?" When I went into the next seminar, the adults were encouraged to find a place in the room to be still before the Lord. I sat for what seemed like an eternity and wept. God's words, "If you love me, you will obey me," came into my thoughts. What was God trying to tell me? I'd been trying to obey him. After all, I was a missionary. I'd given up my life for him.

Next, the Holy Spirit spoke to my heart with words that pierced the very depths of my soul.

"Do you trust me?"

Of course I do.

"No, Natalie. Do you trust me?"

Things began to come into focus for me. If I truly trusted God, then I would surrender to his will, even if that entailed more suffering. Could I do that? Did I really trust God enough to surrender to suffering? I wept and wrestled with God—until, at last, I gave up.

I prayed to the Lord the hardest prayer I'd ever uttered: "Lord, I want to trust you. My spirit is so weak. Forgive my unbelief, and give me the faith to trust you. Even if it means more suffering will come into my life, I ask you to make me more like you." I got down on my face before God and cried until the leaders asked us to leave the room.

I went outside to call and tell Michael about my encounter with God. The moment he answered the phone, I knew it had returned. I could hear the depression in his voice. NO!

"Michael, are you depressed again?" I asked.

Through the tears he sighed and answered, "I wanted to surprise you. I came off of all my medications at Thanksgiving. I was feeling so much better, I really believed God had healed me. I wanted you to see how well I was doing without the medicine, only I'm not doing well. I'm worse."

I returned home to a very melancholy husband. He'd spend all day in bed. When a good friend called to check on Michael, I told him the depression had returned. We called the psychiatrist, and Michael resumed taking his medications. Every day for two weeks, our friend came over in the morning to pray with Michael and to encourage Michael to get out of bed. As soon as the friend would leave, Michael would either crawl back into bed or move to the couch.

As frustrated as I was with Michael for coming off of his medications, I also had a strange peace. I knew that God was with me. Ever since my encounter with God at Passion, I knew that God had not forsaken us. He was molding us into his image, refining us in the fire.

A couple of weeks later, we shared with the church the lessons learned at Passion. For the first time, I shared with them about the encounter I'd had with God as a result of Francis Chan's talk.

"I felt like I was in a wrestling match with God. I am so tired of hurting, but I really do want to be more like Jesus." I said, "My life has been hell the last few years, and I don't know what tomorrow holds. I don't want things to get bad again, but what I do know is that no matter what happens, God will be with me." No one really understood the significance of my statement. However, as best they could, the people in church that night hugged me and promised to pray. I went home feeling very loved.

I truly meant every word I said. I was not facing this life alone. God was with me.

Five days later, I found the frightening message from Michael on my answering machine.

At the time, I truly thought Michael was getting better. The week had started with a small victory. Michael went with me to pick up dinner. This was huge! It was the first time he'd gotten out of the house in two weeks. I went to bed thinking we'd made progress. Michael had not only gone with us to get pizza, but afterward, he went to visit a friend. I thought perhaps his depression was finally going to disappear.

He had spent a lot of time playing with Jorjanne this week. I'd watch him laugh with her. He would smile as he watched her giggle. He read books to her. He tickled her. He seemed to be enjoying life again.

Then I hit *play* on the message machine.

"Natalie, I just wanted to tell you how much I love you." said Michael. "No matter what happens, I love you. You mean so much to me, and I wish I could be a better husband to you. Tell Jorjanne that her daddy loves her and always will. I love you. Bye."

It felt as though my world was spinning. When I had left the house that morning, he told me he was going hiking. He wanted to spend some time alone with the Lord. I thought that was a good sign.

So what was this ominous message all about? Overcome with emotion, I called our friend who had been visiting Michael every day.

"Mr. Bob, I'm not really sure what's going on. I got a message on the answering machine from Michael, and I have this gnawing fear that he was trying to tell me goodbye. I'm afraid he's going to try and hurt himself."

Mr. Bob thought for a minute and asked, "Do you want me to call the police so that they can look for him?"

We agreed that this was the best option. If we could just get Michael home, then we could take him to a hospital to get help.

Time continued to tick by with no word from Michael. I was getting really nervous. Where was he? Why hadn't the police found him? I prayed and prayed for him during those long hours. Throughout the day, I repeatedly called his cell phone, to no avail. Around 6:00 p.m., he finally answered.

"Michael, I'm so glad you answered. Where are you?" I began. He sounded frightened.

"I'm not sure." He sounded so confused. This was so unlike him. He knew these mountains like the back of his hand.

"Where did you park?" I asked, searching for any clues to help us locate him.

"I don't remember," he replied.

Getting desperate, I asked, "Well, at least tell me what you can see."

He was quiet for a few seconds and answered, "I can see Mt. Yonah." Michael sounded like a frightened child.

"Natalie, I can't keep living this way. I'm so tired of the constant mood swings. I am so scared. What if I never get better? I can't go on like this. I won't keep doing this to our family. I am so scared." It was the end of January, and the temperature was dropping. Michael was shivering as we talked.

"Do you have a jacket and gloves? It's getting really cold outside," I questioned him.

"No, I don't have any food either, and I'm getting hungry," he answered. I was shaking too now, but not from the cold. Never had I been so afraid.

"How about a flashlight; surely you have that?" I asked.

"No, Natalie. I don't have a flashlight either."

I pleaded with him.

"Michael, please start walking down the mountain before it gets any darker. There are people looking for you. Please, listen for them. I need you to come home. We can face this together. I need you."

Michael's cries were ripping at my heart.

"I'll try, Natalie, but I am so scared. I love you. I really do, Natalie. I'll always love you."

Tears were streaming down my face. "I love you too, Michael. Come home to me, Baby."

Shortly after I hung up the phone, there was a knock at the door. I opened it to find a police officer ready to write a report.

As we spoke, he kept asking, "Are you sure your husband isn't playing some sort of joke? Are you sure you didn't misunderstand? Maybe he is out hiking or camping."

I was furious that he would suggest such a thing!

"Michael is not playing a joke. He is in danger," I cried. "You have got to find him before it's too late!"

I told him what little information I had gotten from Michael about his whereabouts, and he said, "Well, ma'am, we haven't even found his truck yet. We'll continue to look for him, but if we don't find his truck soon, we'll have to call off the search."

Call off the search? Michael was out there cold and alone, terrified of both life and death and they might call off the search? I refused to let my mind dwell on the possibility. I begged the officer to do what he could.

Once again, I found myself on my knees. Not long after the officer left, Jim, the friend who drove me to the hospital when Michael overdosed, and Doug, Michael's boss, came to the house. They shared their concerns with me and sat with me as we waited. And waited. And waited. My mom continued to care for Jorjanne and put her to bed for me.

And we waited.

About nine o'clock, the search party found Michael's truck. I was so relieved! I called Michael's doctor to tell him about the day. He reserved a bed at the psychiatric hospital for Michael that night. I told the officers when they found him that I wanted him taken directly to the hospital and that I would meet them there.

I anxiously awaited their call. Jim and Doug were still waiting with us, and I tried to convince them to go home. "They'll find Michael, and he'll go to the hospital. There's really no reason for you to stay." They both insisted on remaining with me.

We prayed and made small talk as we all anxiously awaited news. Minutes turned into hours. At midnight, still no word. About 1:00 a.m., I finally called the police station to see what I could learn. They told me that someone was on the way to my house to talk with me. About 2:00 a.m., a car drove up. Jim went out into the yard to meet him and I stood, wringing my hands nervously. I opened the door, and to my horror, there stood a man in a cleric's collar.

Without hearing a word uttered from his mouth, I furiously cried out, "No!"

The priest looked at me and said, "I am so sorry. Michael's gone."

Tell me this is a nightmare! Someone, please wake me up! I screamed inwardly. *Michael can't be gone. What will I do without him? What about Jorjanne? His mom?* My mind was racing. On my knees with tears streaming down my face, I began to drill the minister with questions about that night.

We all cried and held each other for what seemed like an eternity. Then it struck me. I had to tell Jane. Michael's mom didn't know. I had called her earlier in the day, and she was waiting at home to hear from me. I wracked my brain, trying to think of someone who lived near her who could go to her. The only contacts I had down there were unable to share with her, and so it came down to a decision: either the police would go to her home, or I would have to call her. I finally chose the latter.

Trying to stifle my fury and grief, with my heart breaking into more pieces by the minute, I made the hardest phone call I'd ever made and called Michael's mom.

"Mama Jane," I said, trying to sound calm, "I have some bad news. The police found Michael, but it was too late."

She screamed, "Oh, God, no! Tell me it isn't true!"

Not hiding my tears, I answered, "I'm so sorry."

We wept together until I could find my voice and I asked, "Do you want me to send someone down to pick you up and drive you here?"

In between sobs she answered, "No, I just want to be by myself right now."

I tried to get some rest. It was about 4:00 a.m. by then. Just as my eyes began to droop, I heard Michael's mom come into the house. How she had driven all the way up by herself was beyond me! I met her in the living room, and we just held each other and unleashed the tears.

Still in shock from it all, I realized that there was still one very important person I had to tell—Jorjanne. How do you share something like this with a four-year-old? I didn't know what to say.

When she woke up for school, I went into her room and hugged her closely.

"Sweetheart, I have some bad news." I got down on my knees so that I could look into her eyes. "Daddy has gone to be with Jesus." She knew Michael had been sick because he'd been in bed for days on end.

"Daddy went hiking yesterday and was very sick. He got lost, and the police went looking for him. When they found Daddy, he was dead."

She hugged me like no one else could, and for a long time, we just stayed there in each other's arms. Every depth of my being ached in those moments, but I held back the tears in an attempt to comfort and protect Jorjanne.

As I prepared to go to the funeral home the next day, I sat on the edge of my bed, thinking about my hellish day. Trying to sort through the chaos in my mind, I decided to journal. When I opened to the last entry, I was astonished to find these words penned in Michael's handwriting from the day before:

Michael, January 26, 2006

Natalie,

I'm sorry I've brought so much grief and heartache into your life. My heart breaks, but I know the tears will stop. And you and Jorjanne's life will go on. You'll find someone who can take care of you and who is more mentally stable than I am. I'm so confused and so lost. May the Lord who brought this disease welcome me into His kingdom where I'll receive a new body and hopefully, a new mind. I'm sorry I'm not strong enough but one day you'll be thankful I freed you from this living nightmare. Tell Jorjanne I love her, and I pray that she won't have this illness.

I Love You!
Michael

I was shocked! I couldn't believe that he had written to me in my journal. He hadn't freed me from a nightmare—he sent me further into the depths! How would I ever live without him? I only wished it was a nightmare—then I could wake up. I couldn't believe the horror of it all.

After a long, hard cry, I regained my composure and joined my family to go to the funeral home for visitation.

I'm not sure how I made it through the visitation. God carried me when I couldn't walk myself. I sensed supernatural strength and the peace that surpasses understanding. Because of Christ's presence at the funeral home, I found the courage to face the next day at the funeral. I couldn't do it in my own strength but, with Christ's help, I'd make it through the funeral.

❧❧

As I stood nervously just outside the door to the church, all I could think about was the step I was about to take. This was eerily familiar. As I looked around me at my family, my mom, with tears streaming down her cheeks, whispered into my ear, "I love you."

I shifted my weight nervously as the doors opened. There, before me at the altar, was my beloved.

This time, I wasn't walking down the aisle as his bride—but as his widow.

CHAPTER 4

Why is it that when a family member dies of cancer, friends rush to offer their support, but when a loved one dies from suicide, people hesitate to respond? Many choose to stay away because of their fear of saying or doing the wrong thing. Yet, during a family's pain following a suicide, it is critical for them to know others care and aren't judging their loved one. Indeed, some of my friends avoided calling me and later told me they had been afraid that they might "fall apart" and upset me. It's unfortunate that I had no way of knowing that, since in the moment, I felt like they either didn't care or were too ashamed of us to talk to me.

During those early days, I needed people to be with me and sometimes to cry with me. I didn't want people who had it all together. I prayed that real people who could relate to my pain would come alongside me and offer support.

Paul writes in Romans that we are to mourn with those who mourn. Even Jesus wept when Lazarus died. Some of the greatest comfort I received during that dark time was when my friends cried with me and stayed near.

During the funeral, a minister encouraged me to hold my head tall. He spoke about Michael as a great man of God. He reminded me that an illness had robbed us of an incredible man and encouraged me to resist feeling embarrassed because there was no shame in my husband having been sick. The pastor told me to cling to the wonderful memories. Because of Michael's relationship with Christ, we are assured that he is now free from all the pain that tormented him on earth.

I needed to hear those words. I had felt humiliated and ashamed. After all, who would want to admit that her husband shot himself? I confess that I still cringe sometimes when I know it will come up in conversation. Still, that pastor's words gave me the comfort and freedom to let go of the shame. Instead, I could trust God to heal my brokenness.

Emotional support was a godsend, but so was the practical help that I received from caring friends and family. When I felt least capable of processing what to do next or handling a task that felt overwhelming, someone would show up and help.

I waited until the morning after Michael's death to share with my daughter, Jorjanne, that her daddy was dead. We were both grief-stricken. Less than an hour later, friends appeared, offering to keep her for the day. It was a monumental relief knowing that she would be protected from things she was too young to understand. On the day of the memorial visitation, another family took her to see the musical *Annie*. I still can't express well enough the emotions I felt when she came home that night, singing, "The sun will come out tomorrow." Even in my despair, I saw a glimmer of God among us.

Another friend kept Jorjanne during the funeral. Even though they were grieving with me, they were willing to set aside their own pain and minister to my daughter during our time of need.

I remember sitting in my living room just hours before the funeral, sharing with people who cared. One of them asked me what my favorite comfort food was. I had never really thought about that, but I told her that sometimes I crave Zero candy bars. Not long after that, she left with another friend, and when they returned, they brought me a bag full of Zero bars. They had gone to every gas station and bought all they could. This meant so much to me and continued to minister to me in the weeks that followed.

There were many, many other times when I felt God's presence in the kindness of people around me. For instance, a dear friend stayed with me the entire first week after Michael died, and she answered phone calls. It was too painful to repeatedly explain what had happened, so she did it for me. She also addressed and mailed notes of thanks for me. That was huge! My heart was broken, and my brain was fried. I was emotionally incapable of writing stacks of letters to those who deserved my gratitude, so she intervened for me.

Because I was a stay-at-home mom, there were financial concerns. I was frightened because there would no longer be an income, and I wasn't sure how I could quickly replace it. There were bills to be paid, and I had no job. While I was at the funeral home, I received notification that his life insurance may be invalid since the cause of death was self-inflicted. How would I pay for the funeral? I was consumed with worry.

In a surprising and incredibly generous gesture, Michael's employer picked up the expense of his funeral. When I was told, I was shocked and relieved.

It humbled me to know that they cared about Michael and me so much. It was an act of God's grace, and I felt comforted to experience such loving care. My family and friends felt like the hands and feet of Jesus to me during those first few months. I would have been lost without them.

Our church recognized the need for swift assistance and set up a bank account to help. In order to process the necessary paperwork, I had to go to the bank within days of my husband's death. I fought to keep my composure while I made financial decisions that would impact the future. I was so glad my mom went with me. Having her beside me gave me courage to face the day. She was also able to clearly process what seemed muddled to me in the midst of so much confusion and grief.

There seemed to be no escape from the details that demanded my attention and inspired fresh occasions to mourn.

When Michael's death certificate arrived, it was not subtle about the cause of death, and it devastated me to see the specifics in writing: "Death by gunshot wound to head." I was given his personal effects from the coroner, and when I saw the newly missing arm of his eyeglasses, I felt that I would surely collapse all over again. The grief felt like more than I could bear. I just wanted the world to restore itself to normalcy and for my daughter to have a daddy and for me to grow old with my husband, like all the fairytales promise.

Yet curling up and refusing to face our new reality was not an option. Even as I struggled to deal with loss, I also had to confront my own shame and fury. Each time I had to present someone with a copy of the death certificate, I felt embarrassed. Did the cell phone company really need to know that I was canceling his account because he committed suicide? Why was it necessary to show evidence of his death to the electric company, and why did I have to pay a new deposit in order to change the power bill over to my name? It wasn't their business how my husband died. Each time a new person would view it, they would look at me with pity, which left me feeling shamed all over again.

It never occurred to me, at the time, to take someone with me to handle the logistics of Michael's death. I just wasn't thinking clearly about much of anything. Surely, I reasoned, I could go to the phone company by myself. Little did I know what fierce pain those small things would cause!

When the time came to clean out Michael's closet and all of his belongings, a group of ladies from my Bible study came over to assist me. Facing that difficult task was so much easier since I was surrounded by friends who cared. They didn't pressure me in any way. Those ladies let me talk when I wanted to talk. They cried with me when I needed release. They left me alone when I needed to be quiet and reflect. They were heaven-sent!

After the initial shock wore off, letters and cards were balm for my gaping wounds. It was comforting to know that others missed Michael, too, and did not condemn him for the way he died. I wanted people to remember my husband for the amazing man that he was—not as that guy who committed suicide. At his funeral, I asked people to write their favorite "Michael" stories so that someday, I could share them with our daughter. Their tributes were such a blessing to me! When I was overcome with grief and loneliness, I read through their recollections, and even now, I often laugh as they shed light on the precious man I married.

One friend, who wasn't quite sure how to help me heal, was determined to send encouragement. Every morning, without fail, she emailed a different scripture verse to me. Kim gave no commentary—she simply quoted the verse. Her plan worked. It meant a lot to me that she was praying for me each day, and I began to look forward to opening my inbox. What she sent was simple, yet profound, and offered healing to my wounded soul.

The first year after his death was the hardest for me. It was an excruciating cycle of firsts: my first Valentine's Day as a widow, my first birthday without Michael, Jorjanne's first birthday without her daddy, Father's Day, Christmas, our anniversary, and his birthday. It seemed that every time I would begin to get a foothold on coping, a fresh reminder would surface on the calendar. They were all difficult days.

Unlike Kim's encouraging emails, there were well-meaning people who tried to "fix things" by quoting scripture. They would say, "And we know that in all things God works for the good of those who love him."[3] People would assure me that based on that reference everything would be okay. It often felt offensive to me at the time because the assumption seemed to be that

I should automatically, as a Christian, be accepting and look for the good in Michael's death. While many things would eventually shift to become more bearable, all was certainly not okay! My world had collapsed around me, and I didn't know what to do! No one could give me my husband back. No one could restore my daughter's father.

I ached for others to acknowledge my pain and to support me through it. God heard my prayers, and there were some wise individuals who, by honoring my pain, made those "firsts" more bearable. Those who phoned and sent notes of concern and prayer meant the world to me. I felt comforted. It helped to know others hadn't forgotten Michael or me.

I was particularly worried about the first Valentine's Day without him. Knowing this, a precious group of friends planned a special brunch so I would be surrounded with love. The table was brightly decorated, and the atmosphere was lighthearted. We made homemade greeting cards that helped to focus my attention on something other than my loss. They presented a wooden chest that they had decoupaged with one of my favorite paintings as a place to stow special mementos. Then the women each gave me a letter describing their favorite memories of Michael.

Though my heart ached for him, they had transformed a day I had dreaded into a blessing. Instead of focusing on what I had lost, their thoughtful efforts reminded me anew of much that remained special in my life. Left alone, I probably would have wallowed around in self-pity. They made sure that didn't happen.

I have spoken with others who created a Facebook page in memory of the person who passed away. On the page, friends and family can write letters or post messages to the deceased. This can be a safe place to connect people who might be separated by distance so they can grieve together and offer each other support.

Others have wristbands made in their loved one's memory. They wear them as a memorial to the person. When family and friends see others wearing the bands, they can find comfort in knowing their loved one has not been forgotten.

On the one-year anniversary of Michael's death, friends planted a tree at our church in Michael's memory. We gathered together and were encouraged as a minister shared his reflections of Michael. Jorjanne was baptized on the same day, making it even more symbolic for us. God had turned a day of grieving into a day of celebration of life. As we anticipated watching the tree grow, we prayed as a church that we would also see Jorjanne grow in her relationship with Christ. The tree was a visual reminder of God's grace in our lives.

I share all of this with you to emphasize that being present for those who have experienced great loss, especially during that first year, may enable them to survive the unspeakable. I will always remember those who were—and continue to be—there for me.

CHAPTER 5

When a person experiences great loss, grief is a very healthy and normal reaction. I had never experienced such a devastating loss before losing Michael, so I really didn't understand what it meant to grieve. I just thought grief meant sadness.

My counselor explained to me that there are six stages of grief. I came to see that I had actually begun the grieving process while Michael was still alive. His illness had stolen him from me and I knew, even while he was living, that I'd already lost the man I loved.

The first stage is denial or shock. In the first weeks after Michael's death, I'd find myself picking up the phone and dialing his number, momentarily forgetting he was gone. I would think throughout the day about things I needed to tell him. I knew rationally that he was gone, but on a subconscious level, I often forgot. It took time for the finality of his death to penetrate, moving me into another stage in the grief process.

The second stage is anger. It's crazy how we can believe in God's sovereignty and His goodness with our minds, yet our emotions can roar with anger toward Him at the same time. "Why God? Why me?" I must have asked myself this a hundred times. After all, I'd given my life to serving Him. What did I have to show for it? My husband was dead, and I was left behind as a single parent with no job. Was I angry? You bet I was! The crazy thing is that I was afraid to admit I was mad at God. I was a missionary, and I loved God. I thought it was wrong for me to be mad at him. I finally realized that, right or wrong, I was mad, and I was only denying it. I was finally honest with myself and with God about my anger. I found refuge in the Psalms as I read about David's repeated anger toward God and others.

Not only was I mad at God, but I was also mad at Michael and at myself. I blamed myself for not being able to do something to prevent this, and I accused Michael of being selfish and uncaring. Most of my anger toward Michael came while he was still alive. It infuriated me that he would stop taking his medicines. He knew he was sick, and yet he wanted to be well so badly that he refused to admit his illness was chronic. His erratic behavior kept us on a roller coaster much of the time, and there were times that I hated him for that.

One month after Michael's death, I wrote this in my journal to Michael:

> I feel as if half of me has been ripped out. I miss you so much. Today, Jorjanne didn't go to school, and I am exhausted. I need your help. She needs you. Why did you leave us? I know you thought you were helping us by freeing us from your illness, but you were wrong. We need you! No matter how much I pray, beg and plead, you are not coming back, and I hate it. My life seems empty without you. I look around the house and you are there. I go outside and you are there. Everything reminds me of you—only you aren't here.
>
> I'm used to being able to make things better but I can't. Nothing I do will bring you back.

We were supposed to get old together. You stole this from us—if not you, then this stupid illness! I hate it! I feel so much right now that I can't decipher what I am feeling. I'm angry that I have to deal with all the junk and that I have to face life without my best friend. I'm mad that you are in heaven, freed from pain, while I am left here, overwhelmed with hurt.

So much of my life was about you that I don't know who I am anymore. Psalm 56:8 tells me that God bottles our tears; he must have a room full of my bottles because the tears won't stop coming. Oh Michael, you were such a great man! That is what makes losing you so hard!!

I wish I could say that I dealt with my anger all at once and that it didn't return but that wouldn't be true. The stages are more like a staircase. We move up and down the stages throughout the grief process. It is not a linear progression. Six years later, there are still times I find myself angry at Michael about what happened. When I hear Jorjanne crying herself to sleep at night because she misses her daddy, the anger comes rushing back!

The third stage is bargaining. When we realize we are losing someone, we often try to bargain with God in hopes of having more time with the person. I pleaded with God to heal Michael. I couldn't understand why God would allow this illness and, ultimately, Michael's suicide to happen. We were serving God! We were trying to live our lives in obedience to him. I felt like God wasn't keeping his end of the bargain. What I didn't realize at the time is that God doesn't owe us anything. He is God. He is good. He is trustworthy. He is sovereign. These truths later gave me peace, but there were times when I felt like God had betrayed me.

Sadness is characteristic of the fourth stage. Feeling sad is a normal part of the grieving process. However, there are times when grief can trigger depression. When the sadness is severe enough to disrupt a person's life, it becomes depression. The symptoms of major depression include:

- Persistent sadness, unhappiness, or irritability
- Lethargy or fatigue
- Loss of interest in previously enjoyable activities
- Sudden change in appetite (more or less)
- Disruption of normal sleep patterns
- Feeling guilty or worthless
- Moving about more slowly and sluggishly, or feeling restless
- Difficulty concentrating
- Recurrent thoughts of suicide or death [4]

Talking to a trusted pastor, counselor, or doctor can help a person to discern whether his sadness is normal or if depression is beginning to take root in his life.

Naomi, from the Old Testament book of Ruth, is an excellent example of someone whose grief could have turned into depression because of life's circumstances, but did not. Death had taken her husband and her two sons, leaving Naomi with no other choice than to return to her homeland. In Ruth 1:13, Naomi told her daughters-in-law that, "the hand of the Lord has gone forth against me." Naomi discouraged the girls from traveling with her. After all, God seemed to have it out for her. Despite Naomi's words, Ruth solemnly swore to follow her anyway. Once they reached Bethlehem, Naomi changed her name to Mara because the Almighty had dealt bitterly with her. Naomi means "pleasant," whereas Mara means "bitter." If God was in control of everything, didn't that mean that he was to blame for all the bitter things she had experienced? If God loved her, why would he have let these things happen?

When Michael died, I was overcome with grief. Life as I knew it had ended. How in the world would I go on? I did move on, one day at a time.

The same was true for Naomi. While Naomi experienced great hardship and sadness, she did not despair. She made a plan to return to Bethlehem. She kept going; she did not give up. She was uncertain what she would find in Bethlehem, but she knew God was with the people there. She may have known her hope would come from the Lord, but she also blamed him for her current troubles. She blamed God for emptying her life and making her bitter.

Major General Mark Graham and his wife Carol lost both of their sons—within months of each other. They lost one in battle and the other to suicide. The grief of losing two sons almost drove the general into early retirement. He wanted to quit.

The day that Major General Graham was going to turn in his resignation, Carol read to him from L.B. Cowan's *Streams in the Desert*. She read:

> Yesterday, you experienced a great sorrow, and now your home seems empty. Your impulse is

to give up amid your dashed hopes. Yet, you must defy that temptation for you are at the front lines of battle, and the crisis is at hand. Faltering for even one moment would put God's interest at risk. Other lives will be harmed by your hesitation, and his work will suffer if you simply fold your hands. You must not linger at this point, even to indulge your grief. [5]

Realizing that God still had a plan for their lives, the Grahams decided to remain in the Army family. Much like Naomi, they began to move forward in the midst of their pain.

This leads us to the final two stages: acceptance and transformation. Once we accept our loved one's death as reality, we are able to move forward. We never "get over" losing someone we care about, but hopefully, we get to a place where God can use our loss to transform us and to help others.

The pain of losing two sons has motivated the Grahams to reach out to others who are hurting. The Grahams have pledged to use their son's death to raise awareness in the military to the dangers of untreated depression, post-traumatic stress disorder, traumatic brain injuries, and other mental issues. Losing their sons has caused them to become catalysts in suicide prevention.

If you find yourself overcome with grief, hang in there. Take things one step at a time. Allow yourself to feel. When you want to cry, cry. When you find yourself laughing, enjoy it; don't feel guilty. Let others help you. Don't try to make it on your own.

My brother had the following to say about dealing with Michael's suicide: "I found peace first through Christ who strengthens me. My family and friends were a huge support, as well, since we were all going through it together. You have to have people to talk to about how you are feeling—the questions, the doubts, frustration, anger, and even the peace. Seeing that ministry is still being done through the tragedy helps a lot, as well. I had a man tell me, 'Doug, you will never get over this, but you will learn how to deal with it.' That statement was profound to me and has held a lot of truth for me."

It's also important to take care of yourself physically. A friend gave me a one-year membership to the gym when Michael died, and this was the best gift she could have given me. Not only was it great for me physically, but also mentally. Exercise is a great form of stress release.

In 2010, I questioned members of a Facebook group who had lost family members to suicide. When asked if they felt guilt after losing someone to suicide, numerous people answered in the affirmative. Here are some of their responses:

> Yes, I thought if I had been home, maybe I could have stopped it and maybe my daughter could have gotten more help.

> Yes, I did feel guilt, but in an odd way. I felt guilty for feeling relieved that what our life had become could now be over, that I felt relieved because our life could be more stable. Simply, I felt bad for feeling good. It took at least six

months to identify what this guilty feeling was and then about a year to come to terms that it was okay to feel this way—it wasn't a betrayal. It was not wrong. Nor did I need to feel guilt. It was natural to feel this way—just like someone who had been though a long-term illness would feel—and it's okay.

Some even feel guilt because they did not see the suicide coming. I knew Michael was depressed, but I had no idea how tormented he was until I read his journals after his death. I often wondered what I might have done differently if I had known. The "what ifs" can consume us, and there comes a time when we have to let go of the guilt. We cannot judge decisions we made in the past based on knowledge we have now. We may need to forgive ourselves for things we may have done wrong and cannot change. Recording your thoughts in a journal is a great way to help you sort out how you really think and feel about what happened.

Don't be embarrassed if you need to meet with a counselor to help you sort through your feelings. You have experienced a devastating loss, and you may need help to process things. If seeing a counselor intimidates you, take a friend with you for your first session. Having someone there for moral support can give you the courage to face things you might not otherwise.

For a long time, whenever I thought of Michael, I could only feel intense pain. I would be driving down the road thinking about what to cook for dinner when a song would come on the radio that would remind me of him. The pain seemed to ambush me. Months after

Michael's death, I remember driving by an outlet mall where our youth group had once met. The building had been torn down and all that was left was a parking lot of rubble. I began to sob. This parking lot was like my life—what was once a place full of life was now left in a devastating heap.

It took time but, eventually, I was able to remember Michael with joy. I still have those heart-wrenching moments, but now some of the memories carry with them happiness of a good life. Even now, as I reflect on the hard times, the pain is still there, but it is less intense. This did not happen overnight. Be patient with yourself, and give yourself time to grieve.

We will never forget those we have lost. They would want us to move forward in life and pursue happiness. Michael's last words to me encouraged me to plunge ahead and to make a new life for myself. At the time, I didn't want to hear that, but now I find comfort in his words. There is no shame in moving forward.

I once heard a sermon comparing life to driving a car. When we drive, our eyes focus on the windshield so that we see what is ahead. We occasionally glance into our rearview mirror at what is behind us. If we begin to focus on the rearview mirror, on our past, we will crash. In the long-term, a perpetual focus on what "was" can prevent us from living now. While it is important to remember where we have been, we must focus on the present in order to get where we are going. I realize that losing Michael is part of my story, but it is not the whole story. Ultimately, there is a larger story at work—God's story.

This is evident in the life of Job. Satan came to God, asking for permission to test Job's sincerity. Once God granted permission, Job's life seemed to fall apart. He lost the people he loved most. However, God saw the complete picture. Job's vision was limited to the temporal. Perhaps Job would have responded differently had he known that he was being tested. However, God did not explain Himself to Job, and he is under no obligation to explain his actions today. God is in control and has a purpose for suffering, even when he chooses not to reveal that purpose.

Why did God allow Michael to die? I don't know. I do know that God is still in control and that he wants me to be honest with him. God can handle our fluctuating emotions. He wants us to be real with him; he sees through the masks. Job was not afraid to question God. He fired question after question to God and was discouraged when he received no answer. When at long last God did answer, it was not the answer Job had expected—or wanted. I now realize that even if God explained to me why he allowed Michael to die, the answer would not erase my pain. Through the storm, I did not receive answers, but I did receive the grace to face each new day. Job acknowledged that he did not and could not know all the purposes of God. He realized that he must trust God with his life and its issues. Job had been reminded that God cares. Job didn't receive answers, but he recognized God's presence in his suffering. Knowing God brings security, even without answers.

The book of Job is an illustration of the truth found in Romans 8:28—all things work together for the good of those who love God and are called according to His purpose. This verse is often said as a platitude to those who are hurting, but God meant it as a promise. God may not always reveal His divine plan, but we can rest assured that he has one!

Not only does God have a plan, but he is also acutely aware of our grief. The Psalmist writes, "You have taken account of my wanderings; put my tears in your bottle. Are they not in your book?"[6] Because God is timeless, the tears of His children are always before his face. What an incredible thought! God never loses sight of the tears of his people. What tremendous compassion and gentleness the Father has to keep these tears in constant view. It didn't happen overnight for me, but eventually, joy did come in the morning. You can trust God to give you just enough light for the next step. He will guide you into tomorrow, one moment at a time.

Michael, Jorjanne, and Natalie after
church at Helen First Baptist

Michael, Jorjanne, and Natalie after
Jorjanne's gymnastic performance

Michael's office when he was manic

Family photo taken Michael's last Christmas

Michael in Tallulah Gorge

Jorjanne giving kisses to her Daddy

Michael and Jorjanne, two months before Michael's death

Natalie, Jorjanne, and Michael at an Easter Egg Hunt

Michael at the beach in Gulf Shores, AL

Michael posing for the camera at 3
A.M. during Ellijay vacation

Michael, Jorjanne, and Natalie at Vacation Bible
School soon after Michael's release from hospital

CHAPTER 6

One of the most difficult parts of losing Michael was telling Jorjanne. I dreaded it. It had been hard enough trying to explain his illness to her. When he was manic, she would ask, "Why is Daddy so grumpy?" I would share that he was sick and explain that sometimes, when we're sick, we act grumpy. When he was depressed and wouldn't get out of bed, I'd tell her he didn't feel well. I wanted to protect her from Michael's mood swings as much as possible, but sometimes that was impossible.

Now that Michael was gone, I didn't know what to tell Jorjanne. How could I share such a tragedy with her? Should I share that her daddy killed himself? Would it be best to tell her it was an accident? I was determined not to lie to her. I found myself angry with Michael for leaving me behind to pick up the pieces from his death. Not only did I have to deal with the funeral, finances, and a boatload of other stuff, but I had to be the one to tell our precious little girl about this horrific event. It just wasn't fair!

I've since learned that children are resilient. We need to be truthful with them, but telling them the truth does not necessarily mean giving all the details at once. We need to allow them to ask questions and be willing to give answers. However, we often give too much information before a child is ready for it. Understanding death is a process for children; they will continue to grieve at different stages as they mature.

What we tell children concerning death depends on their age.

At the time of his death, Jorjanne was four years old. A few months earlier, we had lost our family dog, Gabby. Michael died in the wee hours of the morning, so I waited for Jorjanne to wake up before telling her about her daddy's death. My home was already beginning to fill with visitors, so we talked in her room. When she went to bed the night before, she knew her daddy had been hiking and that the police were trying to find him.

I got down on my knees and looked her in the eyes and said, "Sweetheart, the police finally found your Daddy last night, and when they did, it was too late. Daddy died last night, sweetie." I paused for a minute to let the truth sink in before continuing.

"I am so sorry, baby. Do you remember when our dog Gabby died? Remember how we were sad and we all cried. We are all very sad about Daddy. It's OK to cry. You may see a lot of people crying, and that's OK. It just means that they are sad because they will miss Daddy. If you need to cry, it's OK, too."

I couldn't believe I was having this conversation. The night before had been hard enough, trying to shield her from the phone calls and the police visits. I wondered how we'd ever survive.

"Jorjanne, Daddy lives in heaven now. One day we will see him again, but until then, it will be just the two of us. We'll both look forward to seeing him one day in heaven."

At first, she thought this meant Daddy was on a trip and would come home. As time passed and she realized he wasn't coming home, she would ask me if we could go visit him. These were tough times. How do you explain to a four-year-old that she won't see her daddy again on this earth? We read children's books about death, and gradually, reality began to sink in for her that Daddy wasn't coming back.

The first two years were difficult for Jorjanne. She would cry a lot at bedtime, asking for Michael. I would comfort her as best I could and then we would pray and ask God to give Daddy messages from us. At Christmas, his birthday, and Father's Day, we would buy balloons and let them float up toward heaven for Daddy so that he would know we were thinking of him. Sometimes, she would draw him pictures to send with the balloons. These small things seemed to help her stay connected with her daddy.

Children thrive on routine. I had been a stay-at-home mom, and now I had to return to work to support our family. In August of 2006, Jorjanne started kindergarten, and I started working again. That messed up our routine, and Jorjanne did not adapt quickly to the change. Her teachers would tell me how she didn't smile at school and that she was extremely quiet. At home, she seemed content and happy, but it was a different story when I wasn't around.

One night, the tears began to fall as I put her to bed.

"Mama, please don't go. Stay with me. Sleep in my room," she pleaded.

With my heart breaking, I said, "Sweetie, it's OK. I'll just be in the other room. If you get scared later, you can come get me."

She was not satisfied.

"Mama, please don't go. I don't want you to leave me like Daddy did."

I felt like I'd been punched in the gut; it took me a few minutes to recover.

"Jorjanne, you know I love you with all my heart. I don't have any plans to ever leave you, but you need to know that if anything ever happens to me, there is one person who will never, ever leave."

"God is always, always with us. He is with you at school, and he is with you at home. He never leaves us. I don't plan to go anywhere, but if I do, you have grandparents who love you and would take care of you. You will not be alone. I'm here, sweetheart."

This is a common fear for children who have lost a parent. It is important to reassure them that you don't expect to die. Sometimes, it is wise to let the child know what would happen to them if something did happen. The key thing is to address the fears and reassure them that they will be protected.

The counselor at school was a great help to us. I could call her with my concerns, and she made it a priority to meet with Jorjanne. She would play games with Jorjanne, getting her to share her feelings. I was afraid that my daughter might stifle her emotions in an effort to protect me. She didn't like to see me cry. Talking with her counselor at school gave her a safe place to be real without fear of upsetting me.

Once Jorjanne and I settled into a new routine, she gradually adjusted to our new life. Her happy-go-lucky personality returned, and she was soon smiling and laughing again. It did not happen overnight, and I had to work hard not to let things upset our day-to-day routine. As long as she knew what to expect each day, she was content, and her fears that something would happen to me began to diminish.

The years continued to pass, and it became evident to me that I needed to tell Jorjanne about how her daddy died. I had prayed and asked God to protect her from the details of Michael's death until she was old enough to understand the sickness. God answered that prayer; she had never asked how her daddy died. Now that she was older, I needed to tell her before she heard the truth from someone else.

As I prepared to tell Jorjanne how her daddy died, I began researching and asking others whose lives had been touched by suicide for advice. It saddened me to realize how many people had been encouraged to protect their children from the truth by lying. Many well-meaning people did this, but it caused the child to mistrust the very people who were trying to protect him. Others were advised to say nothing. One friend shared with me about how he was in his twenties before he learned that his mother had died by suicide. For years, no one would talk with him about his mother's death. Because no one would share the truth with him, he grew up thinking that his father had murdered his mother; he grew up not trusting his father. All of this could have been avoided had the truth been told.

I was convinced more than ever that Jorjanne needed to hear about Michael's death from me. I asked several friends to pray with me that God would give me the words and the timing to do this. Finally, the time seemed right.

Jorjanne was eight years old and was painting a birdhouse at the kitchen table. I was cleaning in my bedroom, and the Holy Spirit prompted me to tell her about Michael. I joined her at the table and began talking about the book I was writing.

"Do you know what Mama's book is about?" I asked her.

"Yes," she said. "It's about your life."

I continued, "That's right. It's about my life with your daddy. God has been so good to us since Daddy died. We've had some hard times, and some days have been really rough, but God has helped us in so many ways. Mama is writing this book so that others who are hurting will know that God can help them, too. I want them to experience the joy that we have experienced." I braced myself for what I knew I needed to say next. I decided to just say it.

"Jorjanne, do you know how your Daddy died?"

"He was really sick," she responded.

Taking a deep breath, I said, "That's true, honey. Your daddy was very sick. He had an illness called bipolar disorder that affected his brain. Do you remember when you were little, you had an imaginary friend named Sukey?"

She nodded.

"You knew deep down that Sukey wasn't real, but you would pretend that he was there." Again, she nodded.

"Well, your Daddy's brain was very confused. He would hear imaginary voices talking to him, and he would think they were real. One day, Daddy was really, really sad and confused. He heard voices talking to him and he was so confused that he killed himself."

She inhaled deeply and just stared ahead.

"Honey, this is called suicide."

Her shoulders shuddered as she continued to listen.

"I want you to know that your Daddy loved you so very much. He absolutely adored you, and he never, ever stopped loving you. You had nothing to do with Daddy's death. He was very sick. If he had been healthy, he would never have taken his life. Never ever forget how much Daddy loved you."

We talked some more, and I said, "If you ever have any questions about your Daddy and what happened, ask me. I will tell you anything you want to know. I promise to tell you the truth."

She nodded and that was the end of the discussion.

This experience reinforced for me that honesty is worthwhile. I never wanted Jorjanne to feel like I'd lied to her—so I didn't. I have told her the truth in increments that she can handle. As she grows older, she will have more questions, and I will give her the answers. Until then, I don't want to overwhelm her with details she's not ready to hear.

The biggest thing for me in telling Jorjanne was to help her understand that her daddy was sick. He was not thinking clearly, or he would have never ever taken his life. Even when mental illness is not involved, a person who commits suicide is rarely thinking clearly. Survivors share their regrets over attempts they made. They often share how circumstances clouded their vision, so they weren't thinking rationally.

I also wanted to point Jorjanne to God's goodness. Even though Michael's death was a tragedy in our lives, God has given us joy since then. I explained to her that by telling our story to others, God can help them to find hope and peace in the midst of their sorrow.

That is my continuing prayer.

CHAPTER 7

As I reflect on the tumultuous times Michael and I shared, there are some things I wish I had done differently. Sometimes, my behavior enabled him to continue in his downward spiral. I thought I was helping when I went to his office at night to work. I now realize that by returning his work-related emails and phone calls for him and by covering for him when he really messed up, I prevented him from facing the consequences of his poor choices. I had become co-dependent.

Yes, his bad decisions might have caused things to go from bad to worse. Michael may have lost his job, his friends, and perhaps even more. However, falling might have caused him to get the help he needed. Perhaps it could have saved his life. At the time, I thought my world would come crashing down if he lost his job. Now, I know that there are worse things.

There were so many times when I was consumed with fear. I was afraid Michael would lose his job, which would cause us to lose our home, and on and on my thoughts would race. If I could do things over, I would have gone back to work. Michael's manic episodes caused him to go on spending sprees that stretched us financially. I eventually opened my own account from which to pay bills, but I know he resented that the money he earned was going into an account he couldn't control. He could have refused to give me the money and, in time, I think that might have happened. If I'd had my own income, I could have made sure that our bills were paid, without worrying about him overspending or losing his job. I think the additional money would have helped to give me peace of mind.

Unfortunately, at the time, I thought that working was not an option for me. It seemed there was simply too much chaos in my life. In hindsight, that was the very reason why I needed to work. A job would have offered me an escape from the day-to-day highs and lows at home. Instead of dwelling on our problems, I could have focused my time and energy on something productive.

There were times when I had to get away for a few days to collect my thoughts. At one point, I lived with my parents for a month in order to refocus. Maintaining a job during that time would have been difficult. However, volunteering might have been a viable alternative. It would have helped me to see others who were hurting, instead of just my own struggles.

Michael was ashamed of having bipolar disorder, and he didn't want anyone to know about it. I helped him keep it a secret. If we had been open about our struggles, friendships may not have been lost. Broken relationships might have been salvaged if people had understood why Michael was behaving the way he was. By keeping it quiet, we shouldered the weight of this burden alone. We needed others to come alongside us and support us, but they didn't even know we needed help. Eventually, I did open up and confide in a few people. I only wish I had done so earlier. It helped so much to have someone to listen and pray with me. Bringing our pain out of the darkness into the light was a major step in my recovery.

Unfortunately, the Church has fallen short in many instances regarding ministering to individuals with mental illness. Too often, people with a diagnosed psychiatric condition have been told that they are demon-possessed or that they are being punished by God for sin. This only serves to "beat them while they're down."

Many have asked me how they can support someone they care about who has a mental illness. First and foremost, love unconditionally. Let your loved one know that you care about them; don't treat them differently because of the illness.

Michael was so afraid of what others would think if they knew the truth about his bipolar disorder. Fear kept him from being transparent. If someone has the courage to trust you with the truth regarding his disorder, offer support, not judgment. Ask how you can help in the recovery process. Listen. Be patient when they stop taking their medications or relapse. We all make mistakes. Do not cast stones, but practice tough love by not being an enabler (like I was for many years). Be willing to research the disorder and learn about it so that you are better equipped with how to help. Chapter eleven provides a resource guide.

If not for our counselor, I think I would have lost my sanity. She helped me to see specks of sunshine when I was only focusing on the dark clouds. By going to therapy with Michael, I was able to hear his heart. I began to realize that he hated the turmoil his disorder was causing in our marriage. This helped me to be more sympathetic to his outbursts when, otherwise, I might have given up.

Group therapy seemed to benefit Michael greatly during his stays in the psychiatric hospital. Both times, when he came home from inpatient treatment, he wanted to stay connected to a support group. The nearest group was forty-five minutes away. Even though he felt like it would help him, he would inevitably decide that it was too far to drive. I wish I had encouraged him to go. It might have been therapeutic for him to talk with others who were struggling. Perhaps those who shared similar pain could have offered him accountability in taking his medications.

A friend told me there is no way to live life without regret. While I didn't share it openly with my friend, I was inwardly berating myself for missing a major warning sign with Michael.

About a week before he died, I walked into the office to tell him something when I caught a glimpse of what was on the computer screen. He tried to minimize the screen before I could see it, but he wasn't successful. Michael was reading an article about ways to complete suicide.

I asked him, "Michael, what are you doing? Are you thinking about suicide?"

He answered, "No. I'm just researching bipolar disorder and I found an article about the risk of suicide for people with the disorder." Satisfied, I'd left the room.

Now I hated myself for not demanding he talk with me more about what he was thinking. My friend told me, "You can continuously beat yourself up with regrets, but the truth is you didn't know what would happen."

That is so true. As I look back on my decisions, I do so in an attempt to help others—not to beat myself up. I've already done my share of that in the past!

For so long, I felt guilty over the anguish I felt. I was a Christian, and I was supposed to love God and others. Why was I consumed with so much rage? I thought I was disappointing God by feeling this way. I've learned that my emotions were normal. When Jesus was in the Garden of Gethsemane, He cried out to God, pleading for help. He knew that he was about to face the cross, and he was overcome with anguish. He didn't want to go there. He was perfect and sinless. His emotions were not sinful. The key is that Christ was obedient to the Father, even in the midst of intense, personal pain. It was not wrong for me to feel anger. I never used that anger as an excuse for me to do wrong. In fact, feeling angry was a normal part of the grieving process.

In everything, I see the hand of God. It was God's grace that kept our marriage intact. He carried me when I felt like I couldn't go on. In the midst of it all, I kept asking God, "Why me?" Now, I see God using this trial in my life as a means for me to encourage others.

As time has passed, I still ask the same question, "Why me?" Why would God choose to use me to minister to others? After all, our story ended in death. I am amazed how God has used the brokenness in my life to give me unfathomable strength. Suffering is a breeding ground for faith when we begin to recognize that God is at work, even in our struggles. Just as God had a purpose for Job's sufferings, ours were not in vain. Trusting in the sovereignty of God to work all things for good gave me incredible hope.

Thinking again on Jesus's time in the Garden of Gethsemane, I realized that Jesus never asked the question, "Why?" He didn't ask because he already knew the answer. Jesus was facing the cross to atone for our sins. Even though he knew why he was suffering, he was still overcome with sorrow to the point of death. Knowing the reason behind his suffering did not negate his pain. We ask "why" because we are hoping for answers, but even with answers, the heartache remains.

Jesus responded to his pain by crying out to the Father. He fell to his knees and prayed, "My Father, if it is possible, may this cup be taken from me. Yet not as I will, but as you will."[7] He was honest before the Lord about how he felt. Why should we be any different?

There is no doubt that I loved the Lord before bipolar disorder entered our lives. However, I see now that I loved God because of all he had done for me. As a result of our hardships, I have come to love God for who he is and not just for what he gives me. There were times when I felt like God had abandoned us. My prayers seemed to bounce off the ceiling. I faced a crisis of belief. Would I continue to trust a God Who allowed pain that I didn't understand? Yet, trusting God was the only hope I had. Even though there were times I felt forsaken, I had to cling to the promises of His Word.

No suffering is pleasant at the time, but it has the power to benefit us by driving us to our knees in faith. I now see that suffering can be a blessing, albeit a painful one. James wrote in 5:11, "We count those blessed who endured. You have heard of the endurance of Job and have seen the outcome of the Lord's dealings that the Lord is full of compassion and is merciful." God does not always numb the pain of suffering, but he suffers alongside us. Suffering demands endurance, but we do not face it alone.

Several people have asked me whether I would marry Michael, if I could go back, knowing what I know today. I have no hesitation in answering that question. Absolutely! We had some incredible times together. I wouldn't trade those memories for anything. We have a beautiful daughter whom I adore. Even though there were gut-wrenching times, they were not in vain. My relationship with Michael has helped to shape who I am today.

There are some things I would do differently, but I would definitely marry him all over again!

CHAPTER 8

One of the questions that plagued me was whether or not there were warning signs I missed. I knew Michael was discouraged and distressed, but I had no idea how desperate he had become. Unfortunately, some people long for relief from the pain, even to the point of death. Statistics show that three-quarters of those who take their own lives do so while depressed.[8] Predictions suggest that by the year 2020, depression will be the second largest killer after heart disease.[9] If this leads many to consider suicide as a viable option, then we need to understand what is meant by the term.

What is depression? This word can mean different things to different people. Many say, "I feel depressed," when what they are actually experiencing is sadness. Sadness is a natural reaction to life circumstances. It is primarily an emotional state triggered by loss of something important to your well-being.[10] Feeling sad is a healthy response to situations that represent loss or disappointment. The emotions aren't permanent. They come and go.

What causes depression? Is it a medical or a spiritual condition? Some say that it is a negative response to circumstances. There are various opinions on the topic. The simplest way to describe it is as one of three things: a symptom, a disease, or a reaction.[11] Studies show that very few people snap out of depression without treatment.[12]

Sadly, suicidal thoughts can plague anyone, regardless of their background. In the Bible, Moses, Elijah, and Jonah all despaired so greatly that they longed for death to free them from their troubles. If these great men of the faith struggled, we should not assume that those we love are immune. Not everyone who attempts suicide has a mental illness, but many do. Not everyone who ponders suicide will make an attempt. While we cannot read someone else's mind, we need to keep our eyes open to clues that suggest someone is contemplating self-harm.

How can you tell if someone is thinking of killing himself? While there is no foolproof way to predict it, professionals point to the following signs that a person may be suicidal:

- Threatening to hurt or kill himself
- Looking for ways to kill himself; seeking access to pills, weapons, or other means
- Talking or writing about death, dying, or suicide
- Hopelessness
- Rage, anger, seeking revenge
- Acting recklessly or engaging in risky activities, seemingly without thinking
- Feeling trapped, like there's no way out
- Increasing alcohol or drug use
- Withdrawing from friends, family, or society
- Anxiety, agitation, inability to sleep or sleeping all the time
- Dramatic changes in mood
- No reason for living, no sense of purpose in life[13]

We need to be aware of these symptoms, in the hope of protecting those we love. If you suspect someone is suicidal, there are two important questions to ask:

1. Are you thinking about how you would do it?
2. Have you thought about when you would do it?[14]

If the answer to either of these questions is yes, professional help should be sought immediately.

Unfortunately, the worst depressions and most suicides happen on the second, third, and fourth of January.

According to bestselling author Tim LaHaye, "It's the worst week of the year. The affliction cuts deepest in those who are prone to it. The holidays are painfully unfulfilled and have given way to the bleak reality of the winter that lies ahead."[15]

If someone suffers from seasonal depression, he may need to take extra precautions during the winter months.

Once you recognize help is needed, where can you turn? People want to be treated with dignity and respect. No one likes to be told what to do. When it comes to getting help, present the hurting person with options. This empowers the individual with the responsibility for his own recovery. The treatment needs to cater to the individual's needs.

Help is available in various forms. Some people may feel most comfortable seeing a family physician. This is a good starting point because the physician can draw blood work and do a physical to make sure that the symptoms are not the side effect from a physical illness. Family physicians can prescribe medication.

When necessary, they make referrals to a psychiatrist, particularly when the symptoms suggest a person may have mental illness.

Contrary to popular belief, psychiatrists are not doctors for "crazy people." When people make jokes about psychiatrists, it can be offensive to those with mental illness, and continues to promote stigma. Psychiatrists are trained professionals who specialize in treating mental disorders. They are well informed of pharmaceutical treatments, as well as alternative treatments specific to each mental disorder.

For a long time, Michael sought treatment from our family physician. Our counselor finally convinced him to see a psychiatrist, and only then did he get a proper diagnosis. I highly recommend seeing a psychiatrist if the symptoms are long-lasting, due to their training.

Some are not comfortable talking to their doctor but may be open to talking with a pastor. Not only does the person who is hurting need unconditional love and support during this difficult time, but his family and friends may need it as well. Pastors are often available to help. They may pray for all involved and give encouragement from the Scriptures. Some churches or denominations have mental health ministries available.

Other caring professionals, such as clinical social workers, psychologists, and licensed counselors can also help someone who is struggling with a mental disorder or with a suicidal tendency. While they do not prescribe medication, they offer empathetic listening and therapy to equip the person with ways to cope. Michael and I saw a psychologist together, and she was instrumental in keeping our marriage intact. She taught us ways to better communicate with each other, especially when emotions ran high. She also helped Michael recognize his need to see his psychiatrist at times when he was spiraling downward.

Support groups are another avenue some people choose to assist them in recovery. By connecting with others who share similar struggles, people often find encouragement and hope. No one likes to feel desperate and alone. Support groups help people realize that they are not alone in their struggles. Chapter 11 of this book offers more details regarding how to find help.

By presenting your loved one with a variety of choices, he is empowered to take control of his own life. If the person who is struggling is dissatisfied with the care offered from one source, other alternatives give him hope that help is out there. Some people get help from a combination of sources. With the abundant resources available, no one should suffer alone.

There are times when a person is a threat to himself, and inpatient treatment may be the only alternative. This can be a scary time for the person receiving treatment, as well as for family and friends. I was not prepared for what I would see in a psychiatric hospital. I cried and cried after dropping Michael off there for the first time. Despite our fears, the care Michael received in the hospital was vital. He not only got treatment from a medication standpoint, but he was also educated regarding his illness.

I will say that not all mental hospitals are the same. Talk with your doctor. Ask others in the healthcare community. You want to find a place that not only medicates, but also approaches the dilemma from a holistic perspective. One of the hospitals at which Michael stayed would not involve the family in his care. A different hospital communicated with me on a regular basis (with Michael's permission) and involved me in the therapeutic process. Both mental illness and suicide attempts affect the whole family. Therefore, in my opinion, treatment should involve the family.

While he was in the hospital, he did not have to face the daily stressors of life (work, bills, family). Michael was able to focus on his illness and work with caring professionals on a recovery plan. Unfortunately, Michael did not stick with his plan. He did not go to support groups like he intended, and ultimately, he quit taking his medications.

Statistics show that one out of seven severely depressed patients who have experienced inpatient treatment will go on to commit suicide.[16] Suicides often occur as the depressed person begins to feel better. According to psychotherapist Richard Gillett, "In the depths of depression, they may decide to die and as the depression seems to lift they regain enough initiative to carry out the act."[17] In fact, the highest suicide rate occurs during the six to eight months after the symptoms have begun to improve.[18] Unfortunately, this proved true in Michael's life.

Family members and friends should know that the risk for suicide has not disappeared because the depression seems to be improving.

In order to help prevent relapse, you must first identify the cause of relapse. What triggers cause a person to contemplate suicide? Stress and relationship problems are common triggers for some. Others might be the presence or absence of certain medications. Look for patterns and see if you can identify potential triggers. Second, you need to recognize early warning signs. Is your loved one withdrawing from activities that she used to find pleasurable? Is there a change in her sleep habits or diet? Is he withdrawing from social situations? All of these may be early warning signs.

Finally, develop effective interventions. The time to do this is when your loved one is well. Sit down and ask them what they would like for you to do if you suspect that they are in a downward spiral. This could involve encouraging them to go to a support group or pastor about their concerns. They may need to call or visit with their doctor or counselor.

If stress is a trigger for someone you love, they may need to exercise or rest more in order to reduce the effects of stress. Have a plan prepared before a crisis situation. Some professionals call this a WRAP sheet—a wellness recovery plan.

There are also some practical things that you can do to help. One way to help is to develop and maintain a connection with the hurting person. People who attempt suicide are trying to end unbearable pain. The depressed person may feel alone and believe there is nowhere to turn for help. One of the major symptoms of depression is an increased sense of worthlessness. Someone who is depressed may negatively interpret the opinions of others. Consequently, we need to reassure our loved ones that we care when we address our concerns with them. We were created for relationships. When we don't connect, we feel empty. Now is a good time to stress their worth and value to you. Make sure they know how much they mean to you!

Another way to help is to assist those who are hurting in understanding and managing guilt. Many people feel guilty because they fail to live up to their own expectations. Depression causes a lot of doubt and isolation from loved ones and often causes people to have difficulties at work—*if* they are able to work at all. These factors can cause a person to feel great guilt and begin to tear away at his self-worth. Guilt—not being able to forgive oneself—is a major factor in suicides today. Judas committed suicide for this very reason. He had betrayed the Son of God. What remorse must have seized him!

However, it is important to point out that guilt is not of God. The Holy Spirit brings conviction, but not guilt. Conviction leads a person to repentance and change, whereas guilt often paralyzes a person. It is very important to help those who are depressed to deal with their guilt, so that they are not overwhelmed by its tremendous weight.

People with bipolar disorder may also need others to help them to see themselves realistically. Negative or grandiose self-thoughts, depending on the mood, often skew their views. Do not let them believe the lies that stigma may have to say about them due to their illness. Remind them that they were created in the image of

God and that they are deeply loved. Help them to see that they are valuable people with a disorder—the disorder does not define them.

Another strategy for helping depressed people is reminding them of biblical examples of people who battled between fear and hope.

When Michael was down, we found comfort in the Psalms. David cried out to God from his heart on numerous occasions, and I found that I could relate to him. For example, in Psalm 40, David wrote about his extended misery in the pit of destruction. "I waited patiently for the Lord, and He inclined and heard my cry. He brought me up out of the pit of destruction, out of the miry clay."[19] David's experience can offer hope to others who feel stuck in the pit of despair.

When depressed, people tend to isolate themselves. It is important that those in deep depression are not allowed to remain alone. Contact with people who care is an essential aspect of their recovery. William Cowper was a poet who lived with depression as a steady companion all his life. There were times when his depression immobilized him, preventing him from even getting out of bed. He repeatedly attempted suicide.[20] John Newton saw Cowper's tendency to withdraw, and he made it a priority to visit Cowper as much as he could. Newton stood by him through the repeated suicide attempts, even sacrificing at least one vacation so as not to leave Cowper alone.[21] People tend to recover more often when they have a strong support system.

There are times when, in an attempt to protect their loved one's reputation, family members fail to seek help. They often fear that their loved one will be embarrassed and that his reputation will be ruined if others know that he has made a suicide attempt. It is when we are at our lowest that we need help the most. If the person had a heart attack, family and friends would call for help without ever considering other options. Why is it that when people with mental illness threaten to hurt themselves or others, we fail to call for help until the situation is dire? If we would only seek out help earlier, a crisis might be prevented.

We worry what others will think if they find out about the mental illness. We fear that our sister might lose her job if her employer learned of her battle with postpartum depression. If the university knew our son had bipolar disorder, would they work with him in his studies or would they kick him out? Would he be ostracized?

Fear grips us and paralyzes us, keeping those we love from getting help. We hide it in shame, thus adding to the stigma felt by the mentally ill. If someone is struggling with depression, odds are that he has a pretty low self-esteem. By keeping their struggle "hush, hush," we are communicating that something is shamefully wrong—thus heaping on more guilt and shame. We need to get past the stigma and get help. Lives are at stake!

Because stigma often keeps people with mental disorders from admitting they need help, some don't receive any. What must we do to get rid of the stigma associated with mental illness? I think the only way to overcome it is by educating the public about mental illness and by affected people telling their stories. This is one of the reasons I chose to share my own. If you or someone you love has a mental illness, feel *no* shame. It is no more shameful than having cancer or diabetes. Hold your head high! Don't let fear or embarrassment prevent you or someone you love from getting help.

Another barrier that often prevents family and friends from intervening on their loved one's behalf is fear of rejection. If a person is suicidal and you force them to go to the hospital or if you call the police, there is a possibility that they may never speak to you again. Many let this fear keep them worrying in silence. Which is worse—a loved one not speaking to you or a loved one who is dead?

Ever since Michael died, I have resolved not to let fear of someone being mad at me keep me from doing whatever I possibly can to protect them from harming themselves. You can deal with the fallout of emotions after the crisis has passed much more easily if you know that you did everything possible, because of love and compassion, to protect the other person. I don't want to live with chronic regrets.

One thing that I have learned through all of this is the need to allow others to make mistakes. When Michael would come off of his medication, I would nag and berate him for doing this to us again. I think it would have been much more effective to find proactive ways to help him monitor himself. Creating a mood journal has effectively helped many to monitor their progress. If Michael had tracked his moods while on and off medication, he would have been able to see the pattern of ups and downs for himself, without my nagging. Some people simply write down one word to describe their mood on a calendar as a way of tracking. Others use online software, such as www. moodtracker.com, to record their emotions online and the technology charts your moods for you. Once he acknowledged his diagnosis, I expected Michael to follow his treatment plan perfectly. What I failed to recognize was that Michael was not only mentally ill, but also he was human. He would make mistakes. He needed my encouragement to keep fighting and striving for recovery. He did not need me to point out his mistakes.

The key to getting help is hope. Fortunately, "of all the psychiatric illnesses, depression is the most responsive to treatment. When properly treated, 80 to 90 percent of people with depression can be cured."[22] If depression is biologically based, "you can trust that God has some purpose in creating you with a physiology or biochemistry that is faulty and accept that as God's will for you."[23]

When someone is overcome with depression, they often feel as if life is spinning out of control. It helps to remember that God is in control and that His purposes are good and perfect. The depression is not without purpose. While the sufferer may not understand the reason for his hardships, he can find some peace in knowing that God is in control.

CHAPTER 9

Unfortunately, the church has often failed to offer love and support to families and friends left behind after suicide. In the midst of grief, the church has, at times, been guilty of causing more heartache by suggesting that suicide is an unforgiveable sin, punishable by an eternity in hell. This teaching is a remnant of Roman Catholicism, based partly on the belief that since suicide cannot be followed by confession, the sin is unforgiveable.[24] However, there are not any scriptures that support this view.

When most people think of suicides in the Bible, Judas is the first person who usually comes to mind. There are five other people who committed suicide in the Old Testament: Abimelech,[25] Samson,[26] Saul,[27] Zimri,[28] and Ahithopel.[29] The Bible does not mention any punishment that these people faced for their suicidal act. I am not suggesting that God condones this behavior but, surely, if it were unforgiveable, the Scriptures would say so—and they do not. Theologian Karl Barth said, "If there is forgiveness of sins at all, there is surely forgiveness for suicide."[30] I concur.

In studies of people who have made serious suicide attempts, psychiatrists have found that 90 percent said they would not have committed suicide had they waited twenty-four hours.[31] This suggests that a person who commits suicide is acting in a moment of desperation, often due to misguided thinking. However, the Bible teaches in the Ten Commandments, "Thou shall not kill." Suicide is a breach of this commandment and is, therefore, a sin. The Scriptures teach that we are only freed from sin through grace by faith in Jesus Christ. It does not suggest that this applies to all sin, with the exception of suicide. In fact, Jesus said that every sin will be forgiven, except for blasphemy against the Holy Spirit.[32] This seems to suggest that a person's eternal destiny depends solely on their relationship with Christ, not on the *way* that they die.

This should give great comfort to those who are left behind. I have no doubt that Michael is in heaven today because he trusted in Jesus Christ as his Lord and Savior. Michael's place in heaven was secured by the grace of Christ on the cross. The Bible teaches that nothing can snatch us out of God's hand once we have received eternal life.[33] "Nothing" means exactly that—if we belong to Christ, not even suicide can separate us from His love and grace.

While the Scriptures seem sparse regarding suicide, they are full of examples of godly men and women who struggled with bouts of depression. Moses, Elijah, and Jeremiah all dealt with forms of depression. While their depressions were based on circumstances and were not due to a medical disorder, as far as we know, the feelings of despair were the same. Their recovery began when they recognized and submitted to God's sovereignty. When they were reminded that God was in control, they became hopeful.

While reading God's Word and trusting in His sovereignty may not alleviate the symptoms of depression, it can offer tremendous hope.

Moses's Wilderness Journey

So often when trials attack our lives, we cry out in anguish and wonder where God is. We feel that God has deserted us and no longer cares. There were times in Moses's life when his relationship to God appeared to be nothing more than master-servant, with no tangible demonstration of God's presence with him. Numerous times, the Israelites cried out to Moses in the wilderness, asking where God was, and Moses, in turn, brought the same queries to God the Father. Like many of us, Moses felt overwhelmed and inadequate in the midst of his circumstances.

When depression attacks a Christian, the believer may face periods of unbelief. He may doubt that God really cares and question all that he has been taught about the character of God. Eighty percent of depressed patients express self-dislike and low self-esteem, much of which is related to a sense of failure to be the type of person that they felt they ought to be.[34] This is especially true of religious people, and this discontentment naturally leads to doubt and unbelief. This unbelief is normal. Moses, one of the great patriarchs, questioned God—yet look how God chose to use Moses, despite his unbelief. How did Moses deal with his unbelief? He took it to the Lord in prayer.

In Moses's story, God had delivered the Israelites from captivity, yet they grumbled and complained because they were hungry for meat. Moses had heard enough, and he came before the Lord crying out for help. Moses knew his personal limitations, and he was frustrated. He had no meat to feed these people. What was he to do? Moses was lonely, and his burden seemed too heavy to carry. He despaired to the point of death. He said, "So if you are going to deal thus with me, please kill me at once, if I have found favor in your sight, and do not let me see my wretchedness."[35] Moses was tired and longed for deliverance, even if that meant death. Moses had experienced many supernatural things as God's servant. He was the leader of a nation; he even saw the glory of the Lord. How could someone so close to the Lord go through a period of depression?

Depression can be used to serve God's purposes. The periods of doubt in Moses's life ultimately strengthened his faith. God allowed the Israelites to wander in the wilderness for a purpose. He wanted to strengthen their faith and dependence on him. God could have sent them directly into the promised land without the desert experience, but he knew that the Israelites would grow weak and apathetic. He wanted His children to cling to him. Sometimes, God allows suffering in our lives so that we will trust him with all of life.

Moses was not only a God-follower, but also a leader for God's children. Yet, he struggled. In an ideal world, Christians would always know there is hope and know that they can turn to Christ, but in reality, there are times when life seems so hopeless that even Christians struggle to endure. Moses's response in prayer is a positive model for Christians to follow when they are overcome with despair. Despite his feelings, Moses knew that hope would be found in the Father. God had proven faithful to Moses, time and again. Moses needed to meditate on the character of God and on His mighty works. By remembering God's past faithfulness, Moses would find hope to trust God with his future.

ISOLATION: A LOOK AT ELIJAH

James wrote that, "Elijah was a man just like us."[36] He faced the same problems as other men, and, in this case, Elijah had a problem with depression. His pride was shattered, and he became a broken and depressed man. Elijah received word that King Ahab wanted him dead. He learned that he had twenty-four hours to leave Jezreel or be killed. Elijah fled into the desert wasteland. He had been faithful to serve the Lord and had seen great miracles. He expected great things to happen as a result of his faithfulness and was appalled that God would allow King Ahab and Jezebel to seek his life.

I can relate to this. Michael and I were serving God with our very lives; we expected rewards and abundant life to be the result. We were shocked when bipolar disorder began to wreak havoc in our world. Surely, this could not be God's will for us. He had great things planned, as a result of our faithfulness. This disorder could not be part of his plan—or could it?

Elijah sent away his servant so that he could be alone. This behavior is characteristic of someone experiencing depression. Depression causes people to isolate themselves. Satan uses feelings of inferiority and inadequacy to cause people to isolate and pull within, to have as little contact with others as possible.[37] When a person rejects himself, he finds it difficult to enjoy other people.[38] The depressed person's view of himself and the world has been tainted because of feelings of emptiness, the loss of energy and the desire to give up.

Despite what the depressed person may communicate, he or she needs the help of others. Depressed people need the presence of those who care. Sometimes, Christians do not want to reveal their depression because they fear rejection. However, research studies have shown that people with fewer close relationships, a smaller social network, and less supportive relationships are more likely to become depressed.[39] Man was created for relationships with both God and others. God created Eve because it was not good for man to be alone. The same is true today. People need the support of others. The most important thing you can do for someone struggling with bipolar disorder, humanly speaking, is to be there when he needs you. By spending time with loved ones who are struggling, particularly with depression, you reassure them that someone really cares.

Elijah fled to the desert and took refuge under the shade of a juniper tree and prayed for death. Elijah exhibited symptoms of depression, wishing for death, together with loss of appetite, an inability to manage, and excessive self-pity. He was unmoved by visitors— even a visit from God and visions.[40] The most common spiritual symptom of depression is to pull away from God—to feel that God is rejecting you.[41] This sense of rejection is often a natural response to anger. When it is difficult to see God's purpose in suffering, we often demand that God bring restoration, and if God does not, the tendency is to turn away from him.

Elijah was angry. After all, he had just shown the prophets the power of the one true God. He was once strong. Now he was weak and, as a result, he assumed that God had deserted him.

Scripture teaches that Elijah not only ran for his life, but also that he journeyed into the wilderness for a full day before he sat down beneath the juniper tree. Exhausted from his journey, Elijah begged for death. Extreme fatigue had undoubtedly overtaken him at that point. When a person is exhausted physically, his mental clarity is blurred. It is imperative that people who struggle with depression do not neglect their physical and emotional needs. Elijah found much needed rest under the juniper tree.

"There is little doubt that some—perhaps many— of the spiritual and emotional and nervous problems, which servants of God face would be at least much improved by more adequate food, rest, and sleep," according to Vicar Tony Baker.[42] Lack of sleep and poor nutrition will cause the depression to worsen.

Elijah's depression caused him to pray rashly, to complain, to be suicidal, and to react with many other sinful acts. Given his attitude, a divine rebuke was expected. The amazing thing is that there was not one. Elijah was not chastised for his weakness. God met him where he was and called him back to work. God's compassion was magnified in his response to Elijah's depression. God continued to use him, despite his emotional meltdown.

At long last, God sent an angel to Elijah—not once, but twice—and the angel told him to "Arise and eat."[43] The most important reason for someone who is depressed to get out of bed is that some energy, some activity, is important in helping the person to recover.[44] Getting out of bed is a major ordeal for those who are depressed. Elijah was so distraught that, apart from the divine messenger, he would not have gotten up from his slumber, not even to eat. After Elijah rested and ate, he found both the physical and emotional strength to travel forty days and forty nights to Horeb.

Elijah was ready to give up. He had dealt with a conglomeration of fatigue, disappointment, anger, and sadness. But God did not give up on Elijah. In a cave, the Lord came to Elijah and encouraged him. Elijah complained that he was the only faithful follower left. Elijah felt not only fear and despondency, but loneliness. God responded to him, "Yet I will leave 7,000 in Israel, all the knees that have not bowed to Baal and every mouth that has not kissed him."[45] It is astounding to imagine that Elijah knew none of the 7,000 people that the Lord noted. Had he become so caught up in himself that he failed to recognize the other believers around him?

Such self-absorption is another symptom of depression. People in the pit of depression often feel as if no one could possibly understand, much less care. Eventually, Elijah discovered that he was not alone at all and that his comrades were more numerous than he could have imagined. The same is true for many who are depressed, but they fail to see the people in their lives who care because of the thick fog that clouds their vision. Having a caring support system is a crucial element of recovery.

JEREMIAH'S BITTERNESS AND LOSS OF HOPE

Planning to serve as a priest, Jeremiah was called by God to be a prophet. He was to warn Jerusalem of the Lord's coming wrath. Jeremiah did not anticipate that obedience to God would be accompanied with suffering. Jeremiah suffered greatly as he sought to fulfill this task. His lament was so great that he cursed the day he was born.

> Cursed be the day when I was born; Let the day not be blessed when my mother bore me! Cursed be the man who brought the news to my father, saying, "A baby boy has been born to you. Why did I ever come forth from the womb to look on trouble and sorrow, so that my days have been spent in shame?"[46]

Despite his despair, this same man later penned the words of 29:11: "For I know the plans that I have for you, declares the Lord, plans for welfare and not for calamity to give you a future and a hope." How could Jeremiah experience such utter despair and, later, such incredible hope—when nothing about his circumstances had changed? Why? Because behind

131

the pain of human calamity is the faithful presence of God.[47]

In Lamentations, a glimpse is given into the very heart of Jeremiah. He felt as though life had assaulted him with bitterness and hardship. He felt forgotten; Jeremiah felt as though he was chained in some dungeon where God would not answer his cries for help. Many of Michael's journal entries reflect his feelings of abandonment. In the dark night of his soul, he, too, felt neglected by God. Like Jeremiah, Michael thought that his sufferings were because he had been alienated from God's favor. How often are Christians told that their depression is a result of displeasing God? Was this true in Jeremiah's case? Certainly not!

The "weeping prophet" is a perfect example of someone who was obedient to God and yet still suffered greatly. Jeremiah's experience shows us how difficult a life of discipleship and obedience to Christ can be, and it also shows God's presence and grace in our darkest hours. When Jeremiah meditated on his circumstances, he grieved. In Lamentations, he cried, "My strength has perished, and so has my hope from the LORD."[48] When Jeremiah focused on his circumstances, all he felt was despair. In time, God spoke to Jeremiah, and his focus shifted from his present circumstances to the power of the Almighty. Nothing about his circumstances had changed—only his focus. Jeremiah ceased to dwell on his circumstances and began to trust God with the outcome.

Once Jeremiah's attention shifted from his current situation to God's promises, a remarkable transition seemed to take place in his attitude. Jeremiah realized the trustworthiness of God in the midst of his depression. Jeremiah was even thrown into a cistern to die, but no more complaints are recorded in Jeremiah after Chapter 20. God mightily used Jeremiah even during those dark days when Jeremiah wished he had never been born.

Just as Jeremiah had to shift his focus away from his circumstances, those struggling with depression must turn their focus to the Lord. Focusing on the depression empowers it. Meditating on the sovereignty of God offers the sufferer hope. Jeremiah encourages us to trust God as we patiently endure the painful experiences that may come our way. By remembering how Jeremiah meditated on the unfailing love of God while feeling abandoned, oppressed, humiliated and bitter, those struggling with depression can find hope and encouragement during times of distress.

SPIRITUAL BLESSING: PSALM 73

Sometimes, depressed believers struggle to understand why God would allow the hopelessness of depression to overtake them, despite their faith. Depression can be a spiritual blessing, although an unpleasant one. How? Those times of darkness often force people to cry out to God. Millions are pleading with God to take away their pain and, at times, God refuses. How can those who are depressed find hope to endure? According to Paul, "tribulation brings about perseverance; and perseverance, proven character; and proven character, hope: and hope does not disappoint, because the love of God has been poured out within our hearts through the Holy Spirit."[49] God's sovereignty and his Word offer hope to believers who are affected by depression.

All of us must persevere in our own struggles in order to find intimacy with God. There is joy in holding a newborn baby, but it is incomparable to the joy a new mother feels after the travails of childbirth the first time her eyes rest on her new child. She feels a closeness and connection to the child because of the toils she faced to bring the baby into the world. In the same way, the sufferer will come to a greater understanding of who God is because of suffering. A.W. Tozer said this about pain and suffering:

> Slowly you will discover God's love in your suffering. Your heart will begin to approve the whole thing. You will learn what all the schools in the world could not teach you—the healing action of faith without supporting pleasure. You will feel and understand the ministry of the night—its power to purify, to detach, to humble, to destroy the fear of death. You will learn that pain can sometimes do what even joy cannot, such as exposing the vanity of Earth's trifles.[50]

In this respect, suffering can be a spiritual blessing.

In Psalm 73, the writer's beliefs about God collided with his personal experience. He had been taught that God is good to those who are pure in heart, yet he saw many wicked people who seemed to have no struggles and seemed to be blessed. He was a man with a pure heart. This man knew the Word and lived a life of obedience to God. He was a good man, but he was not equipped to cope with his illness. Like many of us, he wondered why he, who had endeavored to live a righteous life, suffered while the wicked enjoyed life. This outcome seems an injustice, and the psalmist was tempted to turn his back on all that he had known and learned about God. Day after day, this vexed and plagued him, leaving him in a state of depression.

However, as the Psalmist wrestled with these apparent inconsistencies, he came to realize that God was all he had. God was his strength and would never forsake him. As he came to recognize God's presence, the psalmist became assured of heavenly protection and guidance. Because of his time of suffering, the psalmist came to understand God's goodness in a significantly different sense. He came to know the Lord as his Refuge. All who turn to him will find him and experience the peace that comes from resting in his presence.

Before Michael's struggle with bipolar disorder and his subsequent death, I loved God because of all he had given to me. Now I've learned to love him because of who he is and not because of what he has done for me. Much like the Psalmist, my relationship with God was enriched and deepened, as a result of the intense struggles that I faced. In his illness, the Psalmist thought he had been abandoned by God, but he later realized that he had never been alone. I, too, have come to experience this precious gift: the presence of God.

If suffering drives a person to God, is it necessarily a bad thing? No doubt, it is not pleasant. Yet, if it allows its bearer to experience the depths of God's love in a deeper and more meaningful way, it is possible that a blessing is part of the plan. We exercise to build muscle. In the same sense, our heavenly Father may permit His children to struggle in order to build our spiritual strength.

C.S. Lewis referred to pain as "God's megaphone."[51] Allowing suffering in our lives is a fail-safe way for God to get our attention. In times of pain and heartache, we tend to cry out to him.

When we are weak, he is made strong. Indeed, his strength covers any pain we may endure.

CHAPTER 10

Days after Michael died, I began asking God to turn my weeping to laughing and my mourning to dancing. People told me that I was crazy and that I just needed to get through one day at a time. While that was true, I didn't want to just survive; I wanted to thrive. Even though it didn't happen quickly, I can honestly say that God has not only restored my joy, but has multiplied it. People tease me, saying that I always smile. The funny thing is that many of them have no idea there was a time when I thought I'd never smile again.

Two months after Michael's death, I went to Mexico on a mission trip. One of our first assignments was to find a place to be alone and spend one and a half hours alone with God. Up to that point, I had filled my life with activity. Every time I got quiet, I fell apart. Jorjanne was with me on the trip, and I was relieved that I could get out of "quiet time" because I would have to care for her. As we were leaving to find a place of solitude, a friend told me that Jorjanne had fallen asleep and that she would watch her while I spent some time with God.

That was a time of fury in my life. I finally unleashed all the tears that had been hovering inside me since the funeral. I had fought to maintain my composure for so long that I was shocked by all the tears and anguish I felt during that time alone. Once I'd been honest with

God and with myself (and felt emptied, emotionally), I decided to go for a walk.

I was walking alone in a huge field when I came upon a plant. It appeared to be dead, blackened, and scorched. As I gazed upon it, I meditated on how symbolic this was of Michael's life, which was now over. However, as I looked closer, I saw a small branch growing from this dying plant that was green and full of life. On its stem were two beautiful, yellow flowers, with more just waiting to blossom. God spoke to my heart in that moment. While Michael's earthly ministry was finished, mine had only begun. God wanted to give me new life and new ministry. He wanted me to grow and bear fruit. The only way for me to do so was to rise above the ashes and remain in the light.

Humbled, I fell to my knees in prayer to God. I was reminded of the story of Jonah in the Bible. God provided a vine to shade Jonah from the harsh rays of the sun, and later, a worm ate the vine. Jonah complained and blamed God for taking away the vine. I didn't want to be like Jonah. I asked God to help me to be thankful for the time I had with Michael. I asked him to help me not to become bitter over losing him.

That was a turning point in my life. I knew that God had not forsaken me. He still had a plan for my life. It amazes me because, even now, whenever I see small yellow flowers, I am reminded of that special time with God. The flowers serve as a reminder of God's abundant love for me. They are God's love letters to me. I pray that beauty will continue to grow out of the ashes.

Since then, my life has taken a new direction. I have grown to know God in a deeper, more intimate way. Before Michael's illness and death, I'd never been in a place of desperation. In the past, I'm sure I gave people "pat" answers to their problems and said I would pray for them (though I confess many times, I did not). Now that I know what it is like to hurt deeply, I am more compassionate to others who are hurting.

I am surprised by the number of people touched by mental illness who call me for help. What amazes me is that they call, even though our story did not have a happy ending. When people are hurting, they want to talk to others who have been there. They want to talk to a real person who is not afraid to be transparent. When Michael was sick, I longed to find someone with whom I could talk, who had walked in my shoes. It seemed there was no one. Today, I can be that person to others.

One way I've been able to connect with others whose lives have been touched by either mental illness or suicide is through the Facebook group, Tears to Joy. I created the group as a place for people to encourage and support each other. When I read comments on the site, I am in awe of the strength of so many who have overcome great tragedies. Others are in the pit of despair, and it is such a joy to see the group embrace them and offer encouragement.

Friends encouraged me to start a blog, and eventually, I gave in to their requests. This, too, has given me a platform to share my story. It's not about me, but it's about giving others hope. Even though Michael's life ended tragically, his story continues. After he died, I prayed, asking God to use his death even more than He used his life. It was a tall request because Michael's life was an amazing testimony in the years he was well. God is answering that prayer as people still call me, years after his death, sharing how his death has impacted them.

One lady told me that she struggled with depression. She tried to self-medicate with illegal drugs, which only took her deeper into the darkness. She had decided to take her life. She went to church one final time to make amends with God before her death. She walked into the church and sat down. She noticed heavy hearts around her. She shared that the pastor began to talk about how this was not an ordinary Sunday because they had lost a dear brother in Christ. The pastor then proceeded to address Michael's suicide. This was the Sunday following Michael's death.

She told me that hearing Michael's story gave her hope. She was able to see a church that loved him and missed him. She saw the need for fellowship in her own life. She ended up giving her life to Christ and joining that church. She frequently reminds me, "Even though I never knew him, your husband saved my life." Even as I write, tears come to my eyes. God brought something beautiful out of something horrific.

In order to better serve others, I have decided to go back to school and pursue a counseling degree. While my experiences give me the ability to empathize with others, the academics will give me sharper tools to help. I want to research prevention and look for ways to help others cope in a healthy manner.

The church has a responsibility to those with a mental illness and to their families. People are desperately searching for help, and many don't know where to turn. Many churches want to reach out, but don't know how. I am currently working with CHIP (Community Health Interfaith Partnership) to develop a toolkit for churches to use to better minister to parishioners who struggle with mental illness. I want to see the church rise above the stigma and reach out to families touched by suicide or mental illness.

If bipolar disorder had not touched my family intimately, my life would have taken a totally different path. Michael's suicide has helped to bring the horrors associated with mental illness out of the darkness and into the light. We hid Michael's disorder for years, but healing couldn't begin until it was brought into the light. Unfortunately, we waited until it was too late.

By sharing our story now, I want to bring mental illness and suicide out of the shadows. We need to talk about these things. There is still a stigma associated with personality disorders. Those who knew Michael were shocked to learn that he struggled with bipolar disorder because he was such an amazing man. His life and death are educating others about mental illness. It has shown that suicide can affect people from all walks of life. It isn't something that influences only the feeble and weak-minded. Michael was a high-functioning individual with a zeal for life. He was the last person on earth who I ever thought would commit suicide.

I see the need for advocacy and education, as well as for care and support.

I cannot be silent.

Losing Michael was like losing a part of me. By fighting to support others, I feel certain that his death was not in vain. By sharing our story and helping to guide others toward recovery, I hope that Michael's death will ultimately save lives.

That is also my heartfelt prayer.

CHAPTER 11

Losing someone to suicide brings additional issues to the grieving process. It is common for survivors to feel embarrassment, rejection, and shame. Many feel like other people may blame them for their loved one's death. I never expected to feel so much anger at Michael for leaving us. I felt like he abandoned us. Grief is devastating enough without all the additional complications.

Losing someone to suicide is more common than we'd like to admit. Researchers at the Centers for Disease Control and Prevention surveyed more than 5,000 randomly selected adults in the United States and found that 7 percent had lost someone to suicide during the previous year.[52] This is heartbreaking for everyone left behind.

It has been six years since Michael died, and at times, I still feel shame and rejection when I tell someone for the first time how he died. I feel like they will blame me, somehow, or they will wonder what is wrong with me that would cause my husband to want to take his life. I know these thoughts are unmerited, but I have had them, nonetheless.

One survivor spoke on my Tears to Joy Facebook site about the awkwardness of social situations.

"One minute, everyone is joking and laughing and, the next minute, they ask you if you have any children," she recalled. "You tell them your son died, and they ask how. As soon as you say that he completed suicide, the awkwardness begins. Things get quiet. They say that they are sorry and someone quickly changes the subject, leaving you feeling isolated and alone."

What help is available to help someone work through the vast array of emotions?

There are more than 300 suicide-survivor groups available around the nation. Survivors of Suicide (SOS) groups provide a confidential place to meet with others who have walked a similar path. It helps to talk with other survivors who can relate to the various emotions you face. You can find a convenient gathering by visiting the American Foundation for Suicide Prevention website at www.afsp.org. Internet-based groups are also available for those who do not have access to a local group.

Many tell me that one of their greatest challenges is going to church after a major life crisis. "Everyone at church seems to have it all together," shared one woman. "I just can't bring myself to put on a happy face and greet others." While some may feel pressured to fit into a certain mold, that is not Jesus's intent for the church. He said, "It is not the healthy who need a doctor, but the sick,"[53]. The church is full of "sick" people (even though some may be in denial).

Going to church after losing Michael was hard. I couldn't "keep it together." I cried almost every Sunday for a year. I would be feeling pretty strong, and the choir would sing a song about heaven. I would lose it. There were lots of times when I ran out of the sanctuary to the bathroom to sob. Most of the time, someone else would follow me and cry with me.

The church allowed me to be real with my pain. No one expected me to "get over" things. They gave me time to grieve. Feeling painful emotions isn't a bad thing. I learned that it is part of the healing process. The church was, and continues to be, my greatest support system.

If you don't find love and support in one church, don't give up. Churches are made up of broken people. We don't always respond to others' hurts the way we should. Instead of getting angry, try visiting a different church. Talk to the pastor and let him know what you need and how the church can help. The church often wants to help, but doesn't know what to do.

In chapter eight, we talked about various providers available to assist families with mental illness. Many people don't have any idea where to begin to look for help. If you need help coping with a mental illness, where should you go? If the grief from losing someone to suicide is unbearable, what do you do with the excruciating pain?

This chapter is designed to give some guidance in the process.

If you decide to see a psychiatrist, don't assume all are equal. You will want to find a psychiatrist who listens to you and who values input from your family. A good psychiatrist recognizes the effects of mental illness on the family and will want to include them in the treatment process. A holistic approach to recovery is essential, and many psychiatrists will encourage counseling and/or group therapy, along with medication.

How do you find a psychiatrist you can trust? A good place to start is asking your family physician to make a recommendation. Also, ask friends you trust, or even your pastor. Contact the psychiatrist's office and briefly interview them. Ask about the doctor's credentials and find out how long he or she has been practicing. Find out if they take your insurance and, if not, whether they have any sort of sliding scale to lower the costs.

The same guidelines are true when looking for a counselor. It often helps to find someone who has similar values to yours. Michael and I met with a couple of different counselors before we found one with whom we were comfortable. It was important to us that our counselor shared our religious beliefs. Ultimately, you must trust the person to whom you turn for help. If you don't, you will not be open and honest, and they will not be able to adequately help you. Take time to make sure your counselor is someone with whom you are comfortable sharing.

In hard economic times, where do you turn if you do not have insurance? A good place to start is by contacting Mental Health America (MHA), an advocacy organization with more than 300 affiliates in forty-one states. MHA works with people to connect them with affordable mental-health services in their communities. Also, contact your local Mental Health Center. They should be aware of local providers and their financial policies. Check with your employer to see if they have an Employee Assistance Program. Many larger businesses have programs in place to help workers get mental healthcare.

Group therapy is a viable option for some people, and it is often more affordable than individualized therapy. You can contact psychologists in your area or ask someone at the Mental Health Center for a referral.

Some churches might offer assistance to members with mental health needs. Many discount stores offer inexpensive prescriptions. Find out which prescriptions are offered at a discounted rate and talk with your physician about low-cost options. Don't let shame or embarrassment keep you from seeking help. The key is to refuse to give up!

Sometimes it helps to go to a support group where you meet with others who share similar struggles. Check with your local chapter of NAMI (National Alliance on Mental Illness, www.nami.org). They offer support groups nationwide. For those who can't find a support group near you, the Depression and Bipolar Support Alliance (DBSA, www.dbsalliance.org) offers online support groups. They also provide advocacy, educational materials, and online mood trackers for those who are interested.

Not all support groups are actually called support groups. I found love and acceptance in a small group Bible study with other women. For me, it was a safe place where I could be vulnerable. They did not judge me but loved and prayed with me through the darkest times of my life. Healing would have taken much longer for me if I had not received such precious, heartfelt interaction with others.

One innovative group, called www.eclubsoda. com, meets for nearly two hours by phone conference line each night, inviting individuals with many life crises to interact and mentor each other. It is led by a mental health counselor who is experienced and compassionate, and is an appealing option for many who are uncomfortable meeting face-to-face or have geographic obstacles to finding competent care.

As you try to recover from the pain, don't run from it. Allow yourself to feel the pain. Don't hide your emotions; face them with courage. Offer forgiveness where it is needed. Forgive yourself for any guilt you may feel. Do not make rash decisions. Seek wise counsel. Live life one day at a time so you don't become overwhelmed. Allow God to carry you when you can no longer walk. Trust Him with your tomorrow.

The prophet Isaiah wrote,

> Do you not know? Have you not heard? The LORD is the everlasting God, the Creator of the ends of the Earth. He will not grow tired or weary, and his understanding no one can fathom. He gives strength to the weary and increases the power of the weak.[54]

We may not understand why life is the way it is, but we can trust God to empower us in and through our sorrows. The passage ends with the assurance that:

> Those who hope in the LORD will renew their strength. They will soar on wings like eagles; they will run and not grow weary, they will walk and not be faint.[55]

May we find the strength to soar once again!

CHAPTER 12

A few days after Michael's death, I received a letter in the mail from a dear friend. I was surprised to discover that the letter inside was written to Michael and not to me. The letter was dated the day of his death. She had written in response to hearing the news of his suicide. The letter inspired me to ask others who had lost someone to suicide to write letters of their own. My intent for including the following letters is that those who are reeling from loss due to suicide will realize that they are not alone in their agony. I also hope that anyone considering suicide as an option will realize that it does not end the pain; it intensifies the pain for everyone left behind.

Unfortunately, my life is not the only one that has been influenced by suicide. It is an epidemic that has touched thousands of lives around the world. In an effort to show how others have been hurt by suicide, I'm including letters to other men and women who completed suicide, in addition to the two letters written to Michael.

When I first started writing down our story, my motivation was to allow Jorjanne to understand what an amazing man her daddy was so that she could fathom the powers his mental illness had over his life, ultimately leading to his death. The more I wrote, my purpose for writing expanded to include others who are hurting due to the turmoil associated with bipolar disorder and suicide. Because this book was originally written with my daughter in mind, I chose to conclude the book with a letter to her.

May these letters be a balm to any open-heart wounds, and may God heal our weary souls!

January 27, 2006

Dear Michael,

Traci Stephens, Josh's mom, called me today and told me about your death. My heart broke and tears fell instantly. "Jesus," I cried, "Oh please, God no!" Just this morning I was sitting at our kitchen table eating breakfast and looking at the Christmas picture of you, Natalie, and Jorjanne that hangs on our bulletin board. Now my mind is spinning, and my heart is sinking. I know that you do not need a letter from me. But I do feel that I need to write to you. I know that you are wrapped up in your Savior's arms right now and that your pain is gone.

I know that you, Michael, did not take your life. Because to you, life was a precious gift from your God whom you lived to serve. At Mercer, you studied about service, and I was greatly blessed to share this time with you. Your love for Christ and others radiated from you. I was so excited to be reunited with you and Natalie again in Helen. You were excited too—about your coming baby and about your work with Georgia Mountain Resort Ministries. But, looking back, I think this is when you began to show signs of your illness.

I have to admit that I am mad at this illness that entered your body and mind because it took away our Michael. It took root in your brain like cancer. You didn't ask for it. You didn't want it. I prayed for your healing as did so many others who love you. Natalie shared the pain of this disease with me. I always felt helpless—not knowing how to console or advise her. She longed for you to be well and have peace of mind again. She wanted her Michael back. She clung to Christ, the Rock, during that time as she is right now. Oh, how I pray for our God to sustain her right now. I must remember that our God is a God of hope. He will turn our tears to joy in His time.

I cannot imagine enduring your loss without faith. Michael, I know that you have been welcomed into the arms of God because you believed in Him and lived to glorify Him and spread the good news of eternal life and salvation through Christ. You were not ashamed of the Gospel of Christ. I don't know why God allowed you to get sick, but I do know that you were a mighty warrior for Him, and you will be rewarded. Natalie, too, is a warrior for Christ, and she too, will be rewarded. I promise to lift her to God in prayer.

I love you, Natalie, and Jorjanne so much. My heart aches for your girls because I know how deeply they love you. I will not despair because our God is a God of *hope*, restoration, love, mercy, joy, peace, *comfort*, kindness, and patience. Please pray with us, Michael, for endurance—show me how to encourage and

151

love Natalie and Jorjanne. Pray that I too, would be unashamed of the gospel and would have a heart dedicated to loving and serving God and others. May I never overlook other people's pain—intercede for us, sweet brother in Christ. You will forever be a saint in my eyes.

Your sister in Christ,
Deirdre Collins

July 28, 2010

Dear Michael,

It seems strange to write words to you that you will never read. Yet at the same time, it seems as though I have wanted to write or say these words to you since you went to be with our Lord. Time has not lessened the sense of loss that I feel in your passing. The emotion of that day has passed and given way to more pleasant thoughts of your life and ministry. Nevertheless, it still seems almost surreal that you are gone.

Every day that I walk out of my office, I look up and see the boomerang that you and Natalie gave to me after the two of you returned from the Olympics in Australia. I mounted it above the door, and I wrote Isaiah 55:11 below it. That's the verse that says, "My word which goes forth from My mouth will not return to Me empty." Seems like a perfect verse for a boomerang— don't you think? Far more than I realized at the time, that boomerang and scripture serves as a constant reminder to me of God's promise. When I get discouraged, that verse comforts me that my labor to preach God's Word is never in vain. Thank you for that gift. I don't think I ever told you how meaningful it is to me.

If you were to stand in front of me today, I would want to tell you two things. I guess it is my way of saying, "I'm sorry."

First of all, I'm sorry that I *underestimated* the devastating effect of your illness. I never thought that being bipolar had thrust you into such torment. I could tell that you were not well and that you were struggling at times, however I never dreamed that it was robbing you of all the joy and peace in your life. You had such an infectious spirit. Your spirit was contagious to all who were around you! It was impossible to ignore that you had walked into a room. Your love for Jesus was so very special and impacting upon us all. I loved having you come around. I'm sure everyone did. I just simply could not imagine there was an illness out there that could overpower that. I was wrong, and I'm so sorry that I did not look closer.

Secondly, I'm also sorry that I *underinvested* my life into yours. I once heard at a Promise Keepers rally a definition of "intimacy." It is *"into—me—see."* I always liked that. As your pastor, I don't think I did that enough. We spent time together, but I didn't pour into your life what I could and should have done. You were so gifted and passionate, I didn't think you needed very much encouragement from me. It's so easy to get caught up in "church work," that we pastors sometimes forget that our work is people. On the day of your funeral I decided I would never make that mistake again. You may be glad to know that I have been mentoring young ministers these past few years. It is a joy. I only wish that I had done that for you. I ask your forgiveness.

In closing, I want to say that Natalie and Jorjanne are doing great. They are awesome, and you would be so proud of them. They are such a huge blessing to all of us at Helen First. God is using them to touch many lives, and I am so honored to be their pastor. I miss you, and I look forward to seeing you in heaven. You went there much too soon.

Until that day, your friend and pastor,
Jim Holmes

August, 2011

Dear Chris,

Do you know how hard this letter is for me to write? Do you have any idea? I was given this assignment by my grief counselor *weeks* ago. And, it's taken me until now to even attempt to put words to paper.

Nobody can possibly understand how I feel since you left me on May 3 after taking your own life. Well-meaning people have certainly tried to understand, but there is nobody around that can fully know or understand the grief I've experienced. Nobody—except me.

After the initial shock, I think I felt anger more than anything. Anger at you. And—if I'm being completely honest—a little anger at God. I was angry because you knew me best in this world and still chose to leave me. You knew the pain and the heartache that I felt after being abandoned by my dad at a young age and then abandoned by my first husband. And—now you abandon me too? How could you do that to me? Didn't you know the heartache that would bring to me? And—you kept telling me to never doubt your love for me. Well, sweetheart, this makes me have some doubt. What happened to the vows we took on our wedding day? Why didn't you open up to me about the emotional and mental problems you were clearly having, as I've since discovered? Don't you think *true* love would have done that? True love would have been bold to admit there were problems out of your control. True love would have confessed your pain to the love of your life. So—yes—I have doubts. How can you love me as much as you say you did and still do this?

What about Anna? She adored you! You became the father to her that she never found in her own dad. Outside of Christ, you were her rock—her security. You broke her heart too. A child of fourteen should never have to feel that they've been abandoned twice, and sadly, she feels the pain of abandonment too. I tell her what I know scripturally—that God *never* leaves us or abandons us. And—while my head knows that—my heart (and Anna's too) is struggling to catch up with what our head knows. It's just too painful now.

I feel you've dumped "life" back on me. I have no helpmate now. Nobody to share my day's events with—nobody to share life's "chores" with—nobody to share our life's sorrows with. Sure, I have friends. But, you were my *best* friend! I could tell you everything! We could tackle anything together.

I miss you. All of you. I miss your laughter and your corny jokes. I miss your cooking (and even the messes that I would clean up afterwards). I miss your fish fries—the result of your hard days of fishing. I miss lying on the couch together in the evenings and watching a little TV and falling asleep in each other's arms. I miss your love!

You loved me better than I deserved and more deeply than I could comprehend at times. Your love was always real. I could see it in your actions, in your eyes, in your smile, in the way you would hold me and kiss me. We were truly *one*!

So, what happened? I ask myself that over and over and over. How in the world could I have missed that you were hurting? I have so much guilt over that. I'm actually not angry at you anymore (most of the time), because now I'm truly sorry. Sorry for not knowing you were hurting and obviously in so much pain. I'm so sad that you didn't feel you could trust me with that pain. Baby, we could have beaten it—together! I was with you for better and for worse!

But now—you get the better—you get heaven. And, I get to battle the worse—life on Earth—without you. Do you know how much pain I'm in? Well, let's just say I'd rather be a quadriplegic than go through this. The pain of the heart has to be the greatest pain that exists. And—you broke my heart—crushed it actually. I'm on this ridiculous emotional roller coaster—never knowing what the next bend or hill is going to hold. Functioning is now my goal. I simply want to just function. Thriving is a dream that still seems too far to reach.

I think the deepest pain lies in the dreams—our dreams—that will never be reached. What about that little orphan boy in Ethiopia that we were planning to take as our own? What about the scuba lessons I was going to take so that we dive together? What about our trip to Haiti next year—to serve alongside Cody and Maria? What about Anna's wedding and the fact she wanted *you* to walk her down the aisle? What about the grandchildren we were going to spoil? What about Venice? What about teaching Anna to drive? What about—? The list is endless because our dreams are endless.

I miss you more than words on this paper can convey. I love you more than my heart can contain. But—the only true solace that I have is in knowing that I'll get to see you again when the Lord calls me home! I praise Him for that!

Until then—I just ache for you...

I'll always love you,
Leah Slack

Dear Mom,

Life is full of challenges. I have often wondered what my life would have been like if you were still in it. Would I have chosen a different path? Would I have had the strength to follow my dreams? Would I have had the courage to take more chances? Would you be proud of the person I have become? Why did you do it?

Unfortunately, I will never know the answers to these questions. Even though I know it wasn't my fault, it will always haunt my soul. I have replayed that scenario in my head hundreds of times. What could I have done differently? What if I had reacted quicker? However, the saddest part is that I have either suppressed my childhood or lost the majority of the good memories.

In life, they say that the butterfly effect means that one small event can set off a chain reaction or a significantly larger change in motion. I have no doubt that my life would have been better with you in it. There would have been so many special moments we could have shared together. I know you would have been a great influence on my life and that your love would have given me the proper guidance through life's trials.

There were so many times that I wished I could go back in time and change that day or at least have had a conversation so that we could have said good-bye properly and gotten some closure. I hope that you have found some peace and happiness. I pray that you are not in pain anymore. I know that you will always live in my heart and that I can feel your presence within me sometimes. I am thankful for that and will always love you no matter what.

I have a new wish, but it is going to have to wait awhile before it comes true. My hope is that I have a long, wonderful life with a lot of great experiences. My wish is that I see you in heaven one day and that your smile is as bright as the sun. Hopefully you are in a better place and God has blessed you with peace and happiness.

My hope is that anyone who reads this letter and is considering suicide will understand the significance of human life and how it affects the loved ones they leave behind. The world is a better place with you in it, and you are loved. Please talk to someone and give life a chance. In the words of the great Jim Valvano, "*Don't give up*—don't ever give up!"

RIP Mom!

Love,
Matt Downey

Dear Daniel,

You always said that every good troop, seaman, or airman knows when he raises his right hand that someday that call to duty may be the last call you ever hear. You always said that the idea that soldiers died in vain was a misnomer.

You had practiced, day after day, drilled until you knew your job and the man's on your right and left. You also said that it wasn't the same from where you all stood as from where we as civilians saw it. This is what you came to do. You swore to protect your country at all costs. That is never in vain. I believed you because I trusted you. I understand that now.

It is much the same with a military wife. When you raise your right hand and take that oath, it is us who symbolically stand there and say that we are willing to stand by you as your wife. We are willing to walk that walk with you. We know what we are signing on to—just the same as you. But I never expected it to be like this. I always knew that when you got on that plane, you might never come back. Every wife knows that her husband may die in the line of service. You just always expect it to happen over there—not in your own home. When someone from the squadron called here and said that you had been injured, my heart dropped. I prayed all night until you called the next day. I was never happier to see you when you stepped off the bus from the flight line at Robins AFB three weeks later. God had brought you home to me.

Or so I thought. The Daniel Burke that I sent over there never really came home. I sent over a loving, quick-witted godly man with a bulldog tenacity and instead received someone far different. Your injury made your current job impossible so you did something I never thought you would do. You took a medical discharge. You were a civilian again with a year. You completely isolated yourself from all of our family—no trips, no holidays, finally even from us in your own home. Your injury worsened, but you were so reluctant to reach out for more help.

You stayed home, taking the pain medicine and saying that there was no help for you. Days and days went without you even leaving the house. Every idea, every thought I had to get more help was met with, "No one can do anything. All they do is give me more pills." But it wasn't. You quit. Why? You were never a quitter. "There was always another door," you always said. But every time I found that door you would slam it in my face.

"They can't help me. No one can. No one understands what I am going through. I don't deserve to be helped for what I have done. God must hate me now."

But none of those are true; I would tell you. There is help—more places—different people who have been there and will understand you. Of course you can be helped. Through Christ Jesus none of us get what we deserve, but we all get His grace. The God that I love and serve would never hate his child. God is Love and in that there can be nothing else. There was still hope, but no matter how hard I tried you turned away from me time and time again. Why?

It has been two years, eight months to the day as I sit and write this. So most days I can tell myself that all the times I prayed for you to be healed, all the candles lit, all the tears cried, that yes, it happened. You are healed. After you died, so many people said, "it was God's will." No it wasn't. I can never believe that for a child of God to take his own life is part of God's plan. It was part of *your* plan. It is what *you* wanted. "It would be easiest, better for everyone," you thought if you did this. Over and over you said those words. It may have been—for you.

And back to those other days that I can't tell myself that it is better this way that you are healed?

Those days, I cry. I cry that I should have found one more doctor, called one more hospital, said one more thing right that I said wrong, and been there for you one time that I wasn't. That if there had been one thing different you would have been healed by God and still be here with us. I would still have a husband. Nathan and Anna would still have a father. And someday their children would still be able to have a grandfather. But you took that away from us.

You stole these things from us. It was only the easy way out for you. Everyone else has had a long road to travel, and that road stretches as far as the eye can see. You left us with the hard path to travel.

I love you always,
Selena Burke

Dear Jorjanne,

There is so much I want you to know, and this letter is only a portion of what is in my heart. First and foremost, I want you to know that you are loved. Your daddy and I loved you from the moment we knew we were going to have a baby. Your daddy used to sit and talk to you while you were in my belly. Shortly after you were born, you heard his voice and turned to look at him. He was ecstatic that you recognized his voice!

Nothing, absolutely nothing ever changed his love for you. If anything, it grew each day he spent with you. Your daddy had a disease, which distorted his thinking. There were medications to help him, but he refused to believe he was sick. He wanted to be healed so desperately that he stopped taking his medicine to prove that he was well. The problem was he wasn't well.

Your dad's disorder caused him to get extremely depressed. His thinking was clouded, and he couldn't remember what made him happy. He was afraid and didn't know what to do. It breaks my heart to think of how hopeless he felt.

The day he died, he wanted to make sure you knew how much he loved you. The last conversation you had with him, he kept telling you how proud he was of you and how much he loved you. You may question a lot of things as you grow older, but never, ever question your daddy's love for you. He adored you! I have no doubt that if your daddy could say anything to you today, he would tell you how much he still loves you.

You have been through so much at such a young age. I am so proud of you and the young woman you are becoming. I pray that God will use this tragedy to make you stronger. I pray that you will cling to your Heavenly Father in your earthly father's absence. I thank God for you. You brought joy into my life on some of the darkest days. When I think of you, my heart smiles. You are a treasure. Don't ever forget it!

Love,
Mama

BIBLIOGRAPHY

Baker, Tony. "Elijah – A God Just Like His." *Evangel.* Spring 2002.

Barth, Karl. *Church Dogmatics.* Volume 3. Ed. G. W. Bromiley & T. F. Torrence. Edinburgh: T. & T. Clark, 1969.

Biebel, David and Suzanne Foster. *Finding Your Way After the Suicide of Someone You Love.* Grand Rapids: Zondervan, 2005.

Carlson, Richard. *You Can Feel Good Again.* New York: Penguin Books, 1994.

Clendenen. Nashville: Broadman and Holman Publishers, 1999.

Clinton, Timothy and George Ohlschlager. *Competent Christian Counseling.* Vol. 1. Colorado: Waterbrook Press, 2002.

Copeland, Mary Ellen. The Depression Workbook. California: New Harbinger Publications, Inc. 2001.

Gillett, Richard. "II Corinthians." *The New American Commentary.* Vol. 29. Ed. E. Ray

Hart, Archibald D. *Depression: Coping and Caring.* California: New York Bible Society International, 1981.

Hunter, Rodney J., ed. *Dictionary of Pastoral Care and Counseling.* Nashville: Abingdon Press, 1990.

Jackson-Triche, Maga, Kenneth B. Wells and Katherine Minnium, *Beating Depression: The Journey to Hope.* New York: McGraw-Hill, 2002.

Kessler, R.C., W. T. Chiu, O. Demler, and E.E. Walters. "Prevalence, severity, and comorbidity of twelve-month DSM-IV disorders in the National Comorbidity Survey Replication (NCS-R). *Archives of General Psychiatry,* 2005.

Kitchener, Betty, Anthony Jorm, and Claire Kelly. *Mental Health First Aid USA.* Maryland: Anne Arundal County Mental Health Agency, Inc., 2009.

LaHaye, Tim. *How to Win Over Depression.* Grand Rapids: Zondervan Publishing House, 1975.

Lewis, C.S. *The Problem of Pain.* New York: Macmillan Publishing Company, 1962.

Murray, Bob and Alicia Fortinberry. *Depression Facts and Stats.* January 15, 2005. http://www.upliftprogram.com/depression_stats.html#statistics.

Piper, John. *The Hidden Smile of God.* Illinois: Crossway Books, 2001.

Rose, Maureen. "Major General Mark Graham: A Legacy of Hope." *TAPS,* Fall 2009. http://www.TAPS.org

Rosen, Laura Epstein, Xavier Francisco Amador. *When Someone You Love is Depressed.* New York: The Free Press, 1996.

Sakinofsky, Isaac. "The Aftermath of Suicide: Managing Survivors' Bereavement." *The Canadian Journal of Psychiatry, 52,* 2007.

Seamands, David A. *Healing for Damaged Emotions.* Colorado Springs: Cook Communications, 2004.

Sproul, R.C. *Now That's a Good Question.* Wheaton: Tyndale House Publishing, 1996.

Swindoll, Charles R. *The Lamentations of Jeremiah.* California: Insight for Living, 1986.

Wemhoff, Rich. *Anxiety and Depression: The Best Resources to Help You Cope. Seattle: Resource Pathways, Incorporated, 1998.*

Wiseman, D.J. "I and II Kings." *Tyndale Old Testament Commentary.* Illinois: Intervarsity Press,1993.

World Health Organization (2005). *Disease and injuryregional estimates for 2004.* www.who.int/healthinfo/global_burden_disease/estimates_regional/en/index.html accessed November 3, 2008.

Endnotes

1   Kessler, R.C. Chiu, W.T., Demler, O. and Walters, E.E. (2005). "Prevalence, severity, and comorbidity of twelve-month DSM-IV disorders in the National Comorbidity Survey Replication (NCS-R). *Archives of General Psychiatry*, 62.

2   Jeremiah 29:11, NIV.

3   Romans 8:28, 29, NIV

4   Mary Ellen Copeland, The Depression Workbook. (California: New Harbinger Publications, Inc., 2001), 12.

5   Maureen Rose. "Major General Mark Graham: A Legacy of Hope." (TAPS Fall 2009), http://www.TAPS.org

6   Psalm 56:8.

7   Matthew 26:39.

8   Laura Epstein Rosen and Xavier Francisco Amador, *When Someone You Love is Depressed*. (New York: The Free Press, 1996), 180.

9   Bob Murray and Alicia Fortinberry, *Depression Facts and Stats*. January 15, 2005, accessed January 9, 2007; available from http://www.upliftprogram.com/depression_stats.html#statistics.

10 Rodney J. Hunter, *Dictionary of Pastoral Care and Counseling*. Nashville: Abingdon Press, 1990), 1103.

11 Archibald Hart, *Depression: Coping and Caring*. (California: New York Bible Society, 1981), 5.

12 Laura Rosen Epstein and Xavier Franscisco Amador, *When Someone You Love is Depressed.* (New York: The Free Press, 1996), 230.

13 Betty Kitchener, Anthony Jorm, and Claire Kelly. *Mental Health First Aid USA.* (Maryland: Anne Arundel County Mental Health Agency Inc., 2009), 106.

14 Maga Jackson-Triche and Kenneth B. Wells and Katherine Minnium, *Beating Depression: The Journey to Hope.* (New York: McGraw-Hill, 2002), 123.

15 Tim LaHaye, *How to Win Over Depression.* (Grand Rapids: Zondervan Publishing House, 1975), 33-34.

16 Jackson-Triche 70.

17 Richard Gillett, *Overcoming Depression.* (Toronto: Macmillan of Canada, 1987), 30.

18 Rosen and Amador 181.

19 Psalm 40:1-2

20 Piper, *The Hidden Smile of God* ,(Illinois: Crossway Books, 2001), 12.

21 Piper, *The Hidden Smile of God,* 96-97.

22 Rosen and Amador 21.

23 Hart 23.

24 Biebel, David and Suzanne Foster. *Finding Your Way After the Suicide of Someone You Love.* (Grand Rapids: Zondervan, 2005), 121.

25 Judges 9:50-54.

26 Judges 16:23-31.

27 1 Samuel 31:1-5, 2 Samuel 1:1-27.

28 1 Kings 16:8-18.

29 2 Samuel 17:23.

30 Karl Barth. *Church Dogmatics,* Vol. III, 4.

31 Sproul, R.C. *Now, That's a Good Question.* (Wheaton: Tyndale House Publishers, 1996), 291-292.

32 Matthew 12:31.

33 John 10:28.

34 Rodney J. Hunter, *Dictionary of Pastoral Care and Counseling.* Nashville: Abingdon Press, 1990), 1105.

35 Numbers 11:15.

36 James 5:17.

37 David A. Seamands, *Healing for Damaged Emotions.* (Colorado Springs: Cook Communications, 2004), 52.

38 Tim LaHaye, *How to Win Over Depression.* (Grand Rapids: Zondervan Publishing House, 1975), 148.

39 Laura Rosen Epstein and Xavier Franscisco Amador, *When Someone You Love is Depressed.* (New York: The Free Press, 1996), 108.

40 D.J. Wiseman, "I and II Kings." *Tyndale Old Testament Commentary.* (Illinois: Intervarsity Press, 1993), 171.

41 Archibald Hart, *Depression: Coping and Caring.* (California: New York Bible Society, 1981), 15.

42 Baker 3.

43 I Kings 19:5,7.

44 Hart 103.

45 I Kings 19:18.

46 Jeremiah 20:14-18.

47 Charles R. Swindoll, *The Lamentations of Jeremiah.* (California: Insight for Living, 1986), 41.

48 Lamentations 3:18.

49 Romans 5:3-4.

50 Timothy Clinton and George Ohlschlager, *Competent Christian Counseling.* Vol. 1, (Colorado: Waterbrook Press, 2002), 23.

51   Clinton and Ohlschlager 23.
52   Sakinofsky 130.
53   Matthew 9:12
54   Isaiah 40:28-29.
55   Isaiah 40:30.